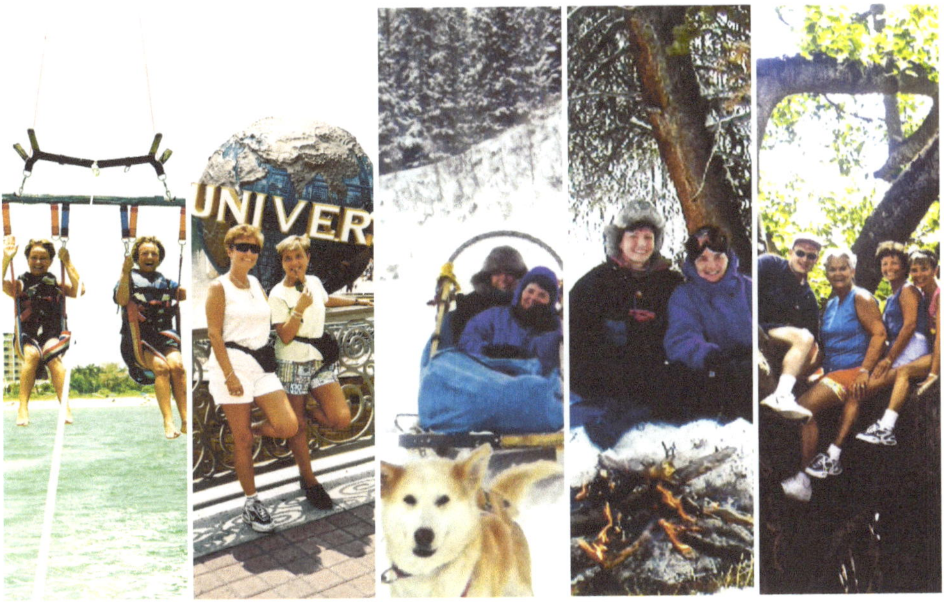

STORYBOOK LIVES

978-1-7398544-6-1 (Paperback)
978-1-7398544-7-8 (e-book)
978-1-7398544-5-4 (Hard Cover)

Printed in the United Kingdom

AEGA Design Publishing Ltd
Kemp House, 160 City Road, London
EC1V 2NX United Kingdom
www.aegadesign.co.uk
info@aegadesign.co.uk

AEGA PUBLISHING

STORYBOOK LIVES

The things we have been privileged to do are definitely fodder for fairytales. Sharing many of our amazing times will hopefully not only offer a glimpse into the wonderful times we have had in this amazing world but also will serve as an invitation for others to step out and make their own memories.

In the course of going to all

SEVEN CONTINENTS, we...

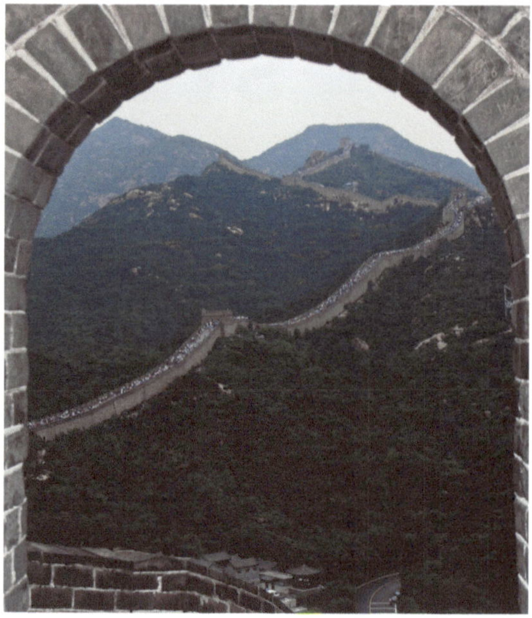

climbed the **GREAT WALL OF CHINA**...

the **INCAN PEAKS OF MACHU PICCHU**...

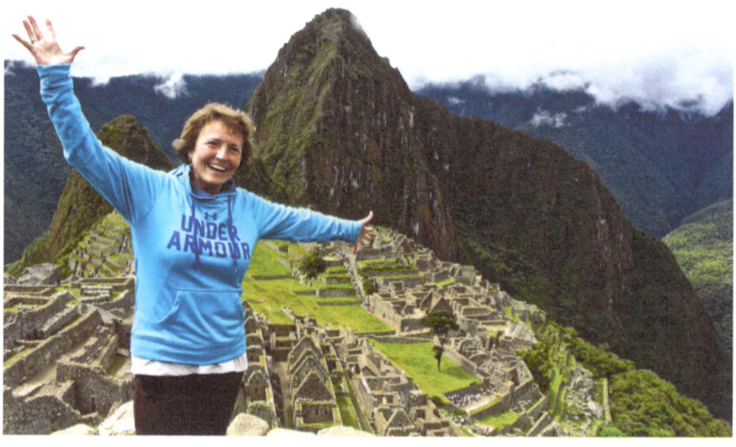

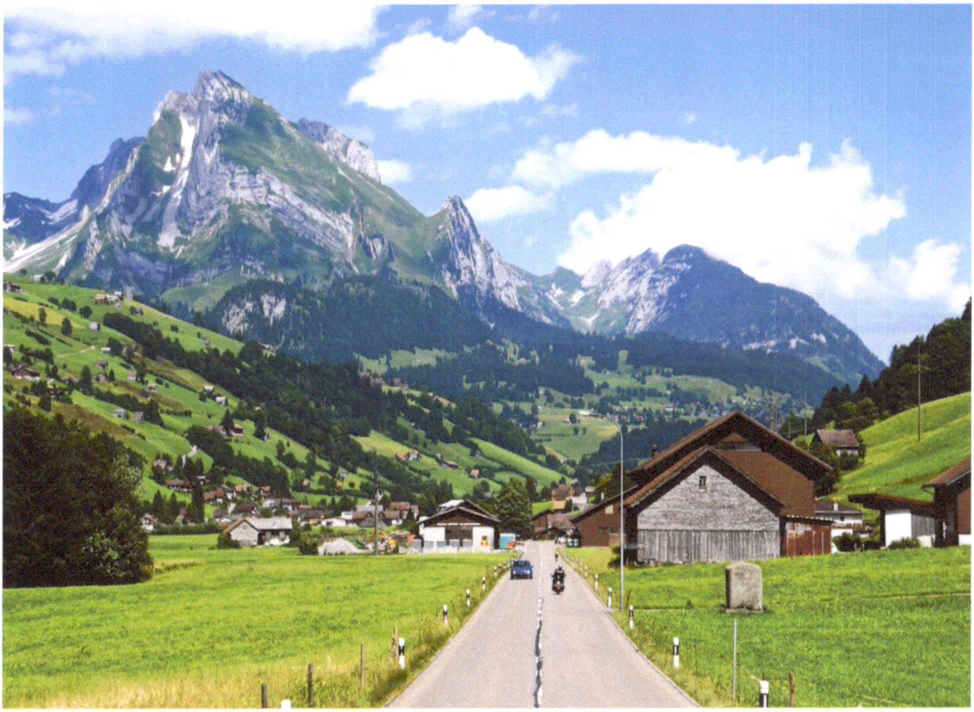

I and the **SWISS ALPS** to Heidi's storybook home...

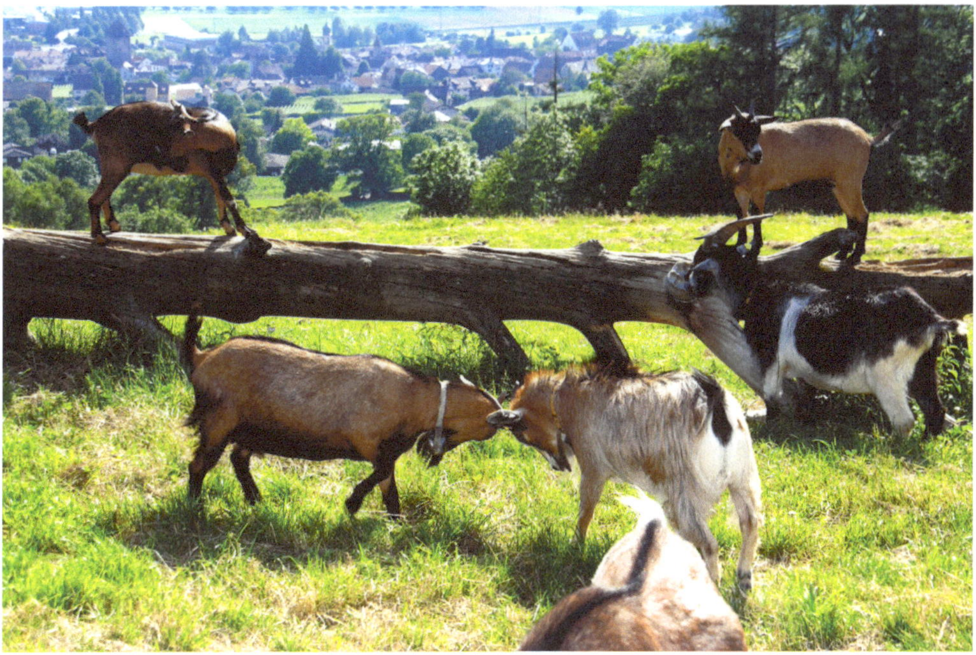

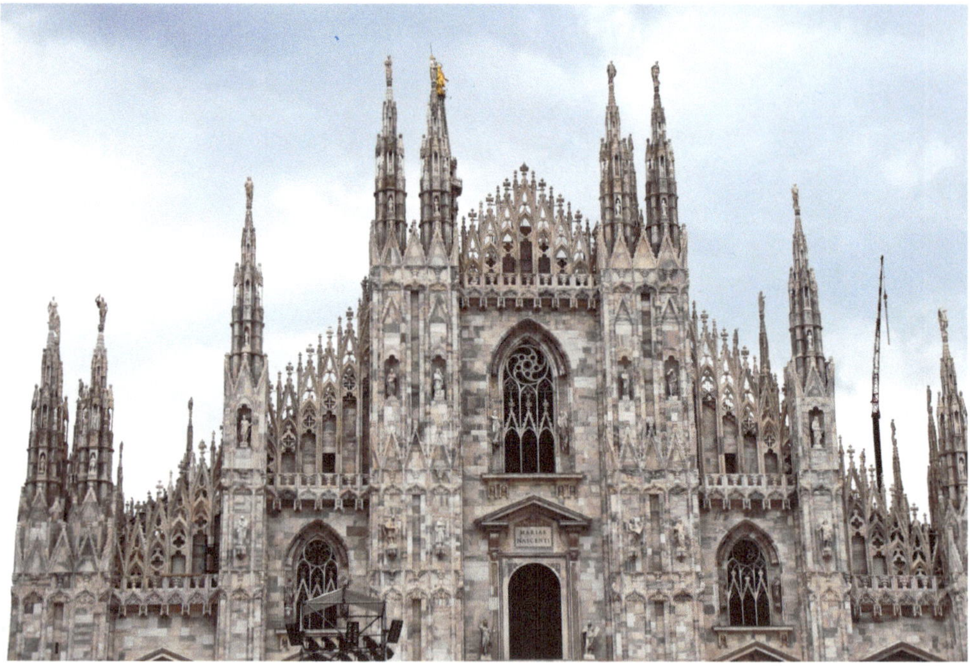

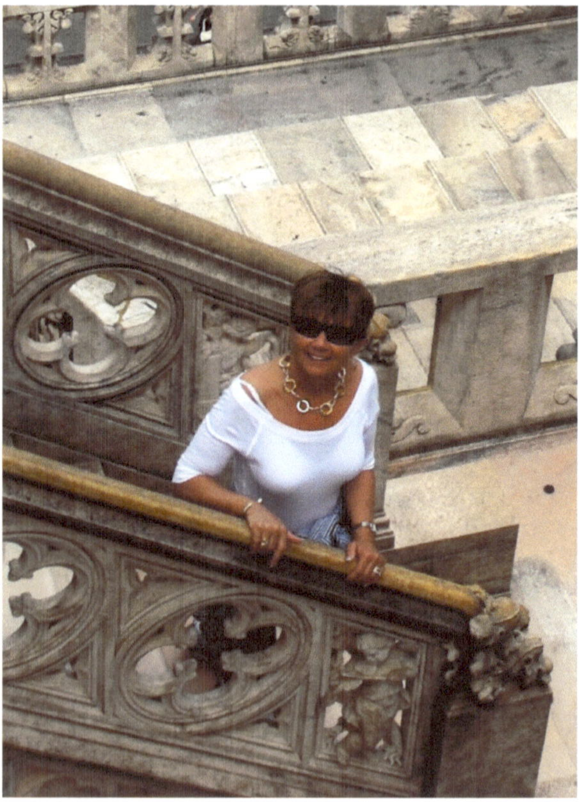

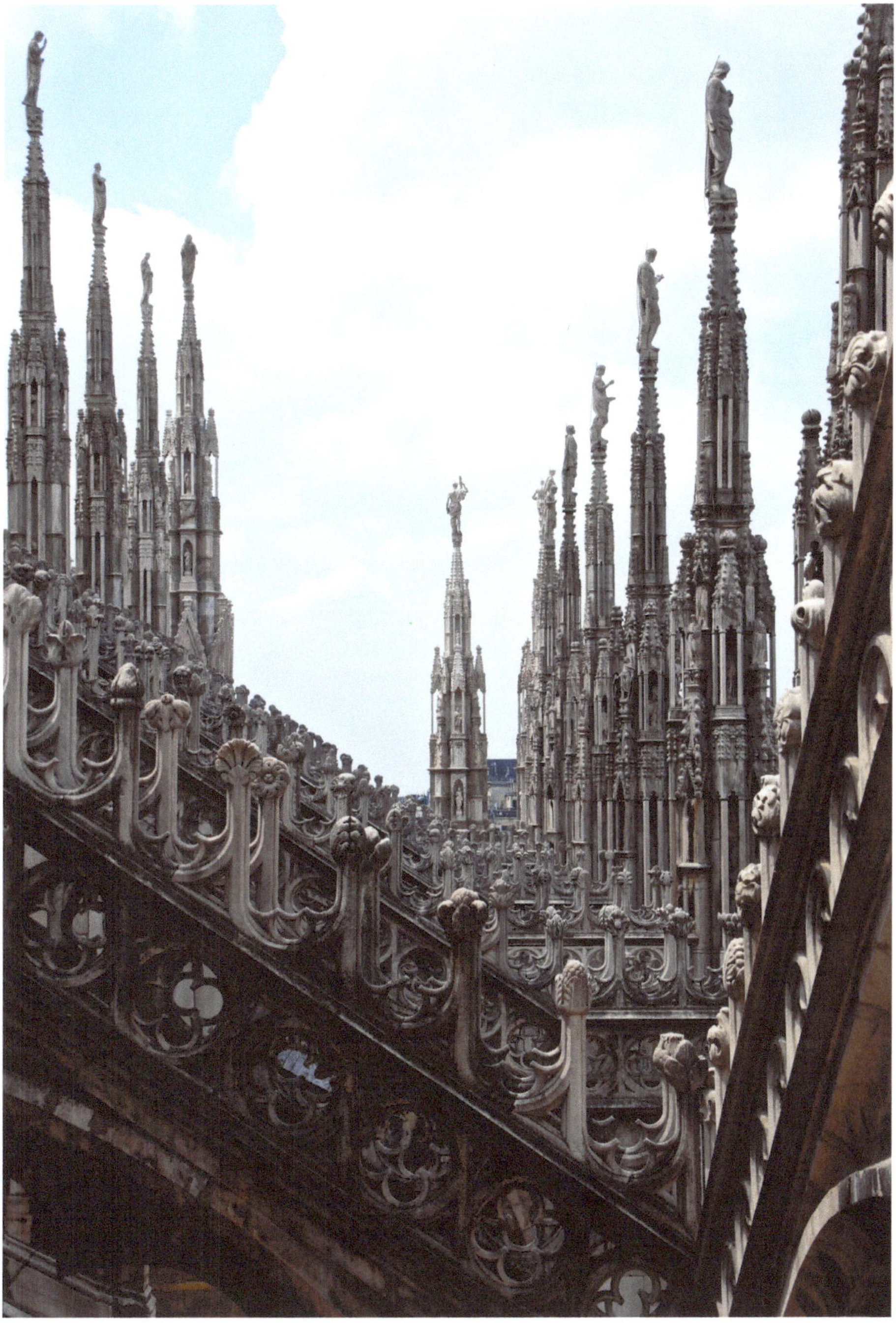

wound our way among the spires of Milan's famous **DUOMO**...

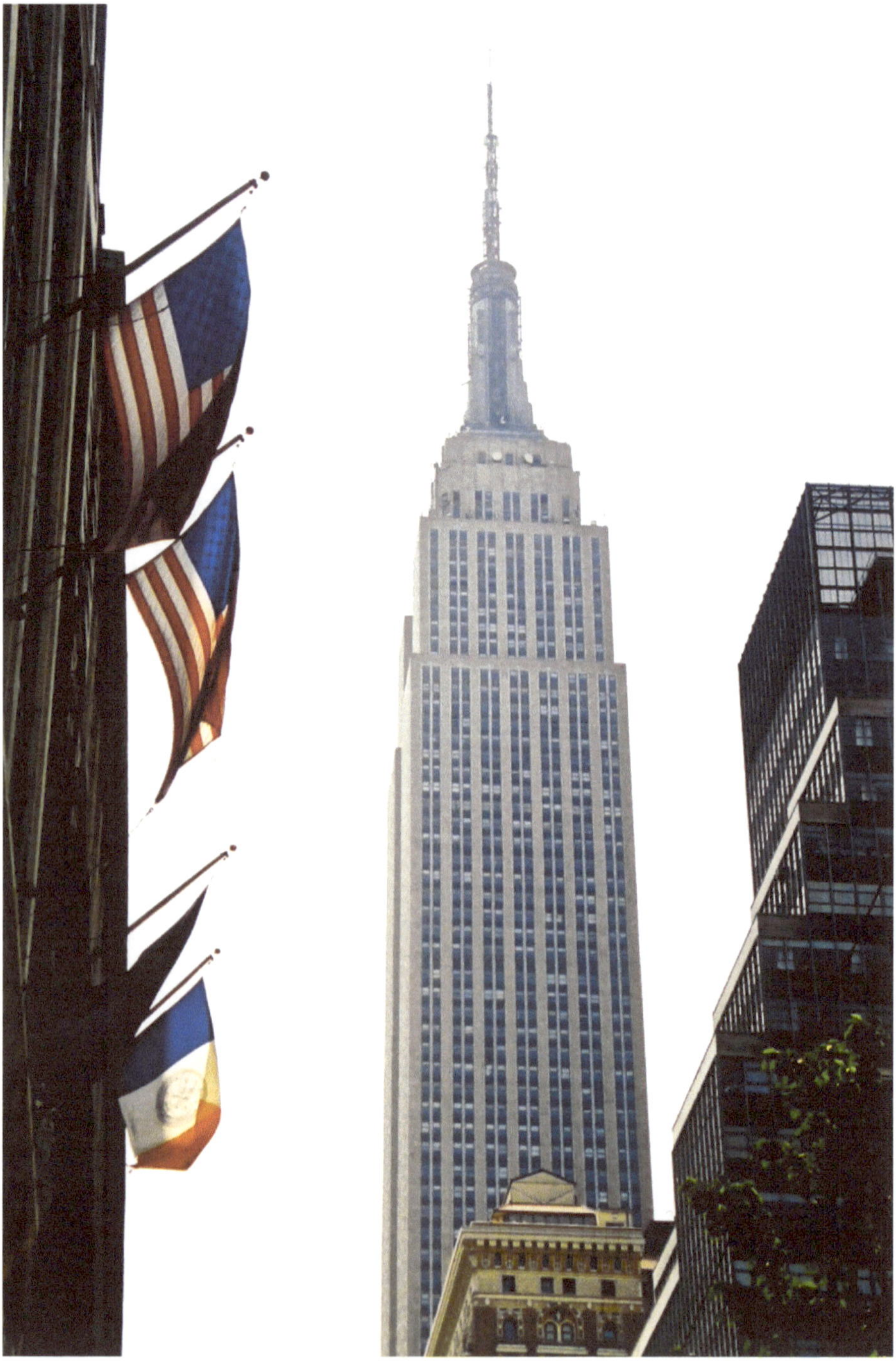

I observed **NEW YORK CITY**
from the top of the **EMPIRE STATE BUILDING**...

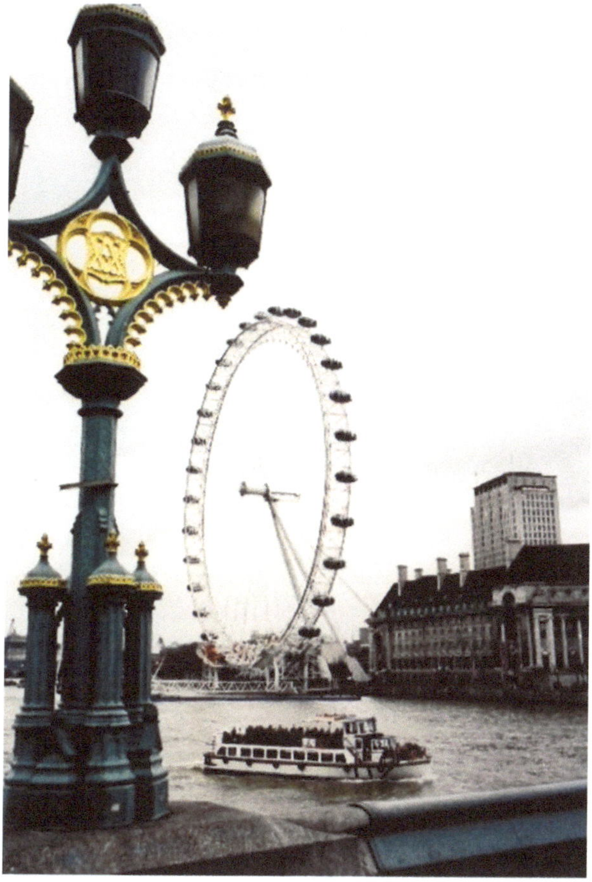

I and London from high in

THE EYE...

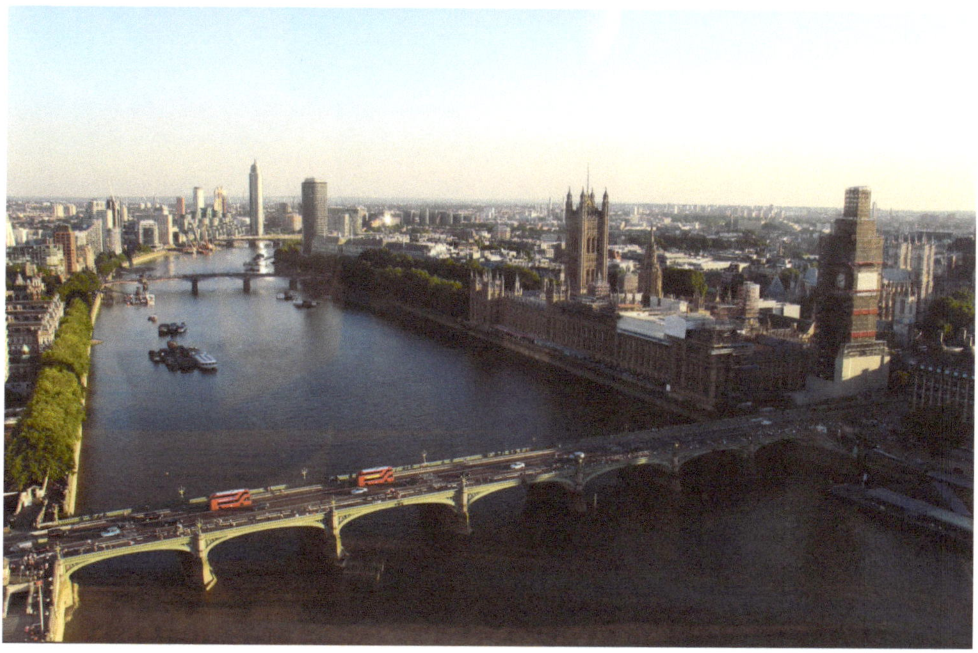

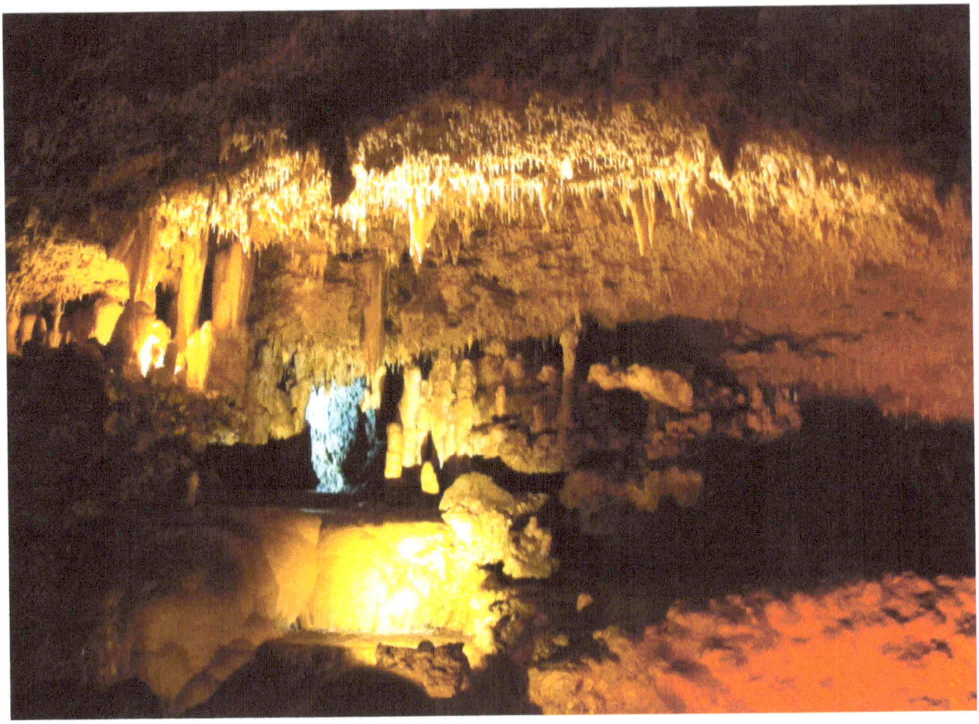

ventured through

BARBADOS'S MYSTERIOUS CAVERNS...

I and went to the bottom of the
CARIBBEAN SEA...

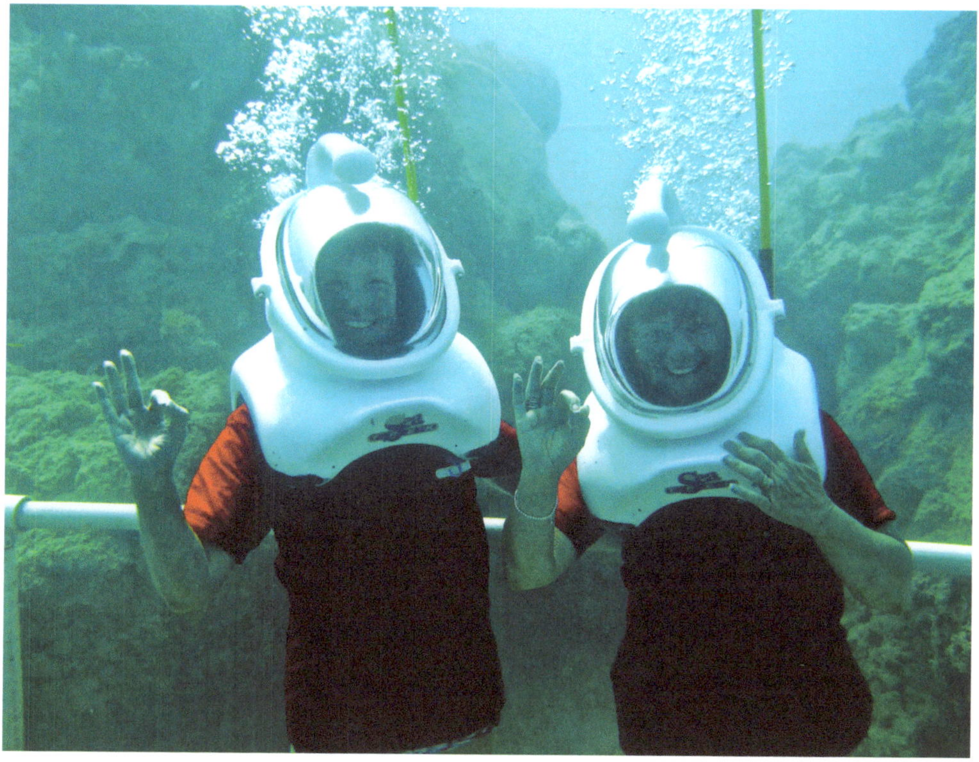

I walked through Beijing's ancient

FORBIDDEN CITY...

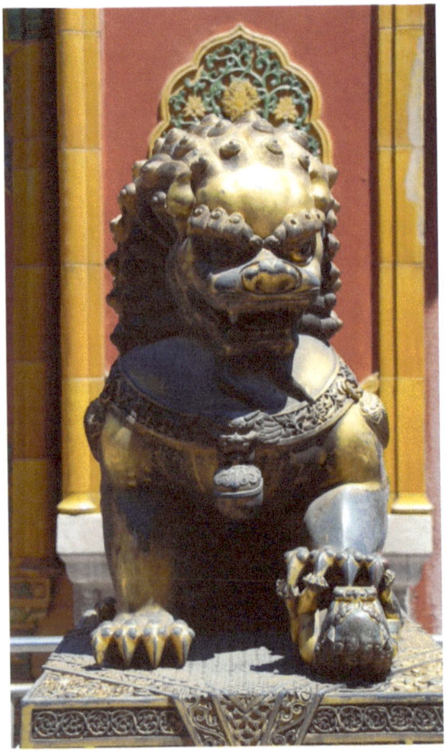

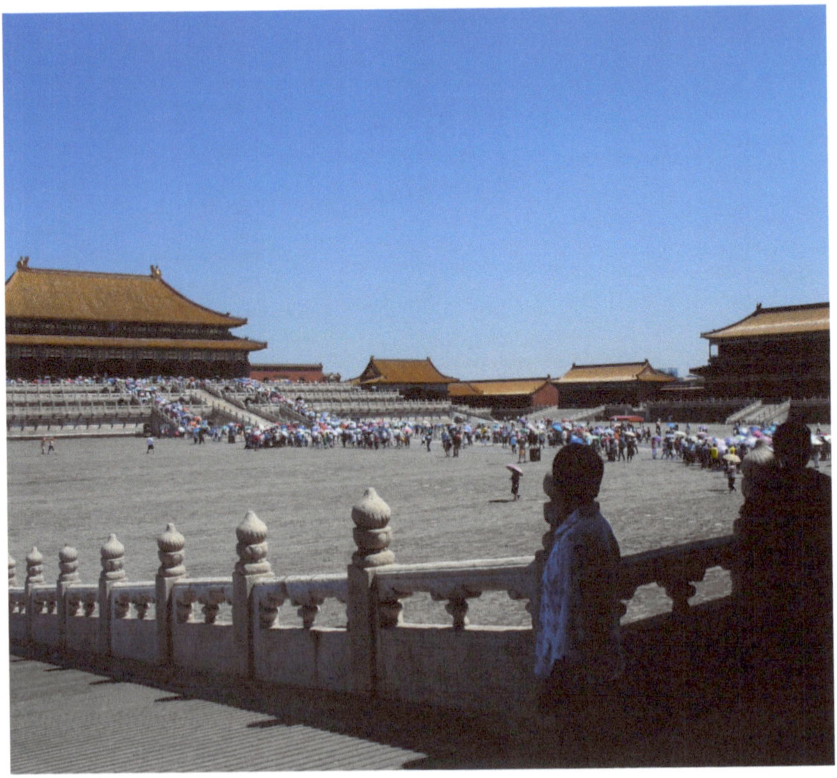

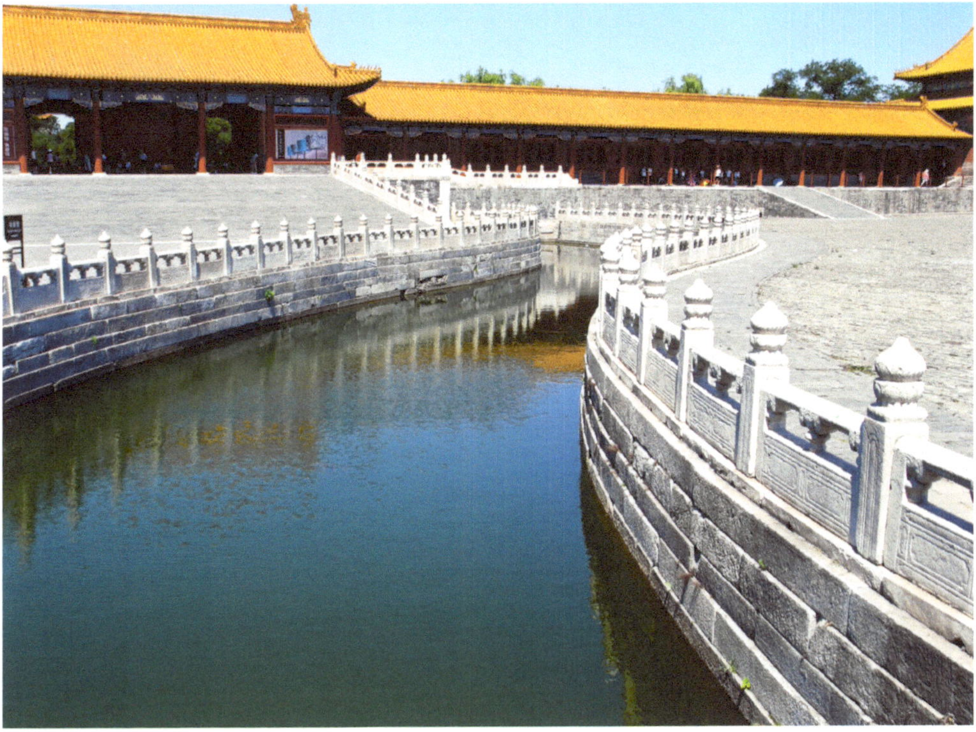

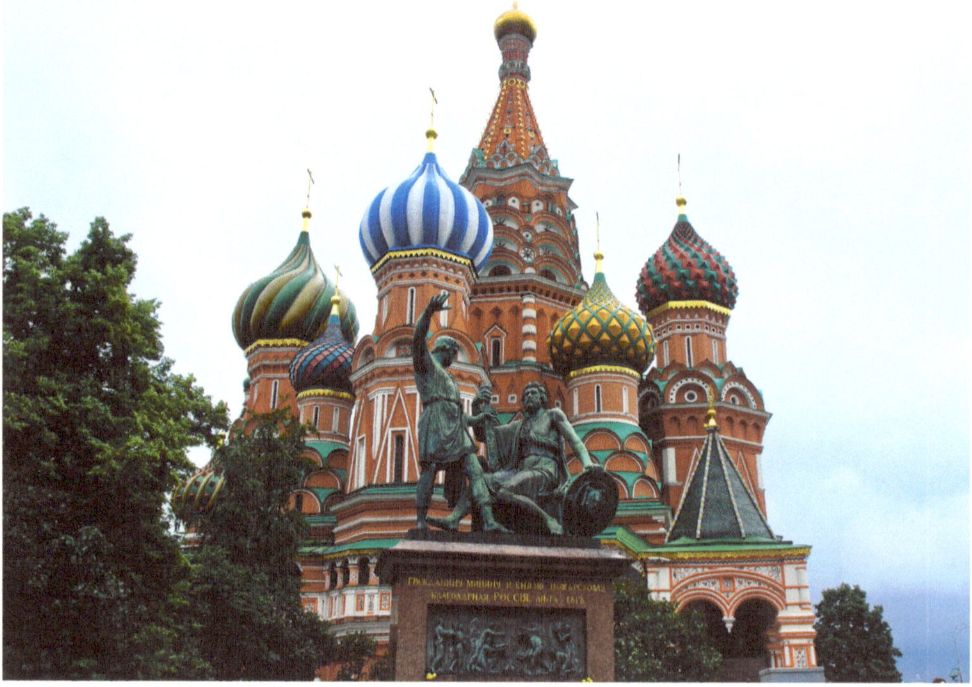

I crossed Moscow's bricked
RED SQUARE...

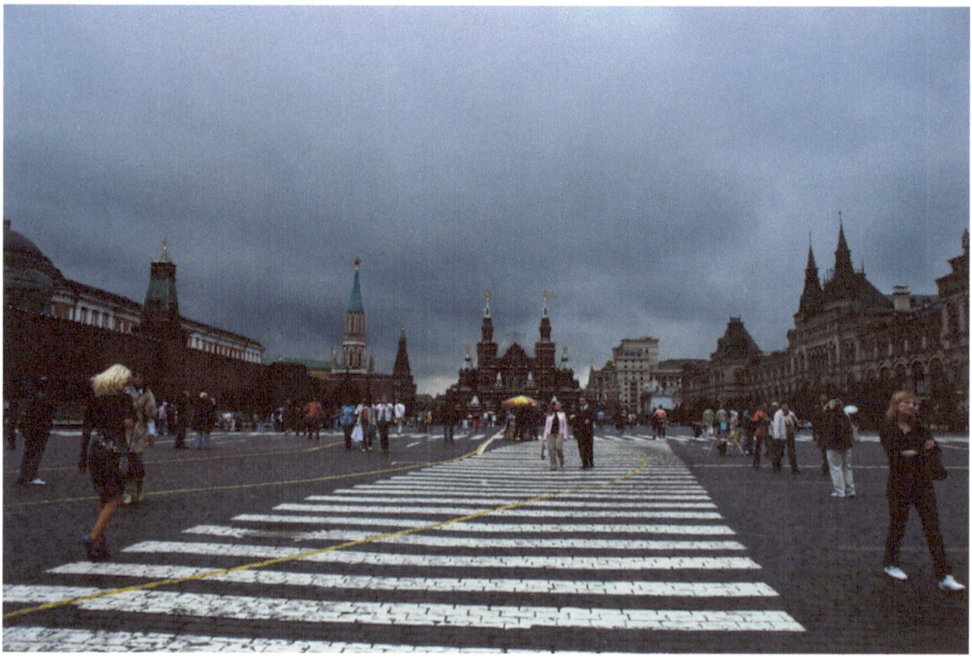

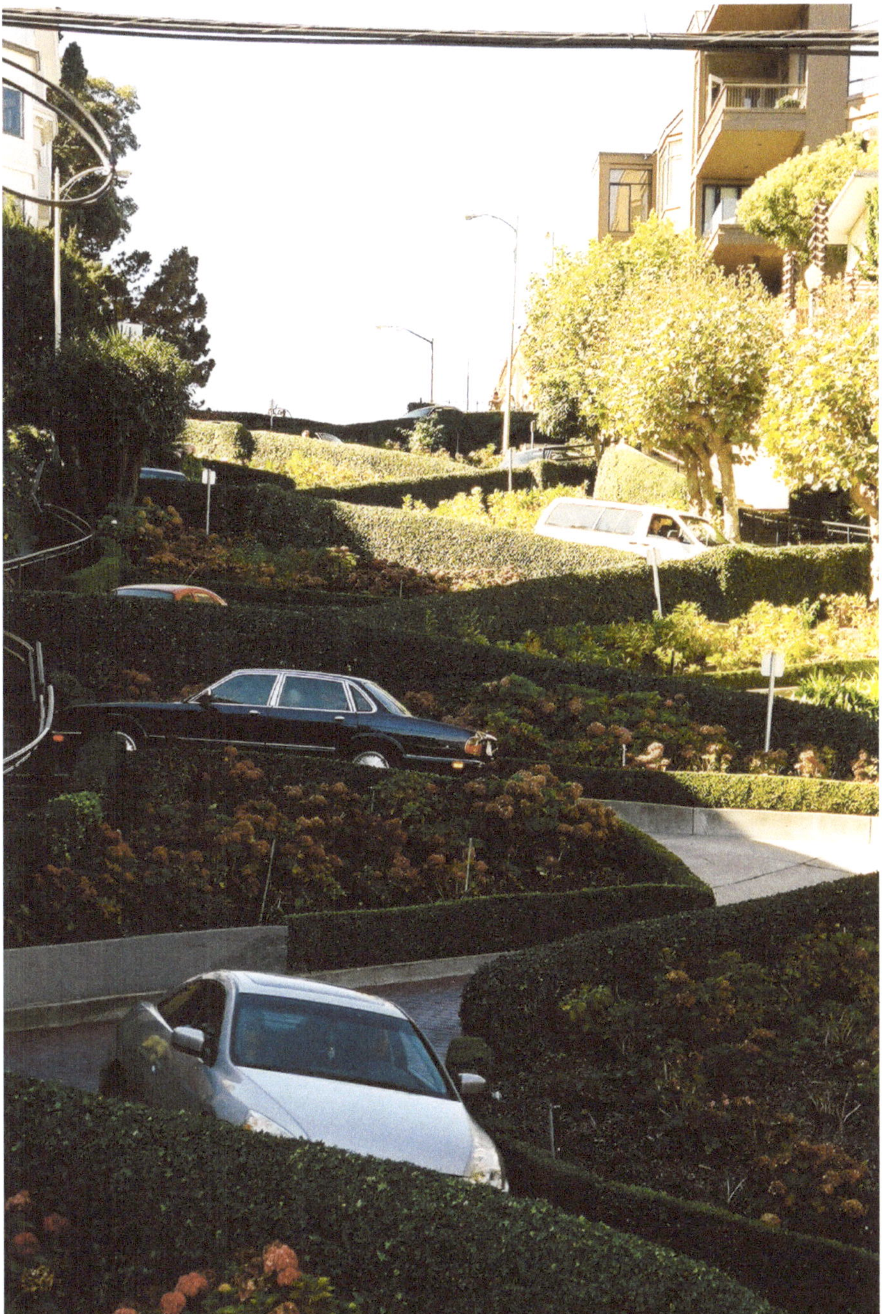

and in **SAN FRANCISCO** walked
down the world's most crooked street...

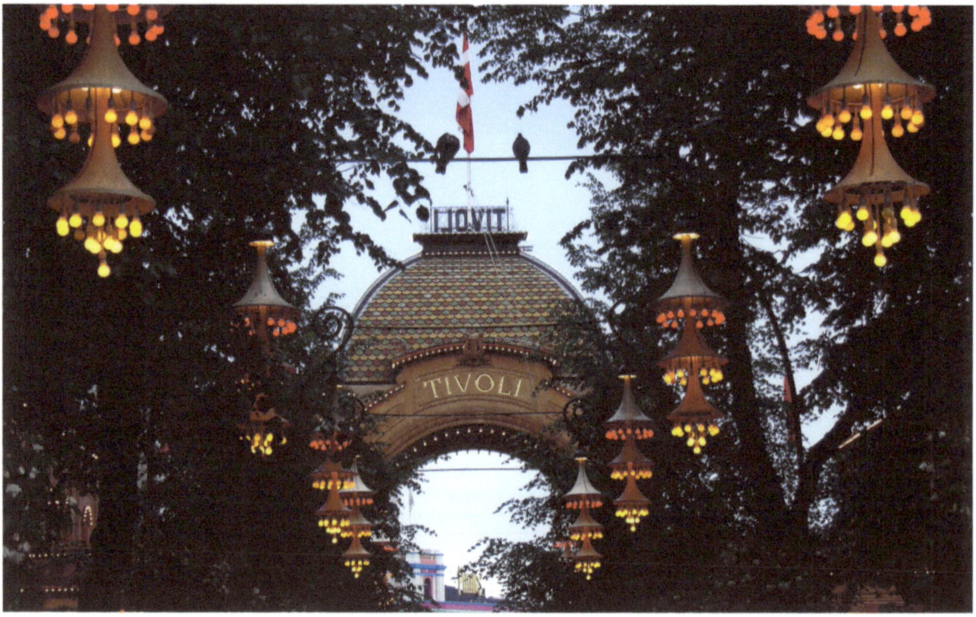

I wandered in amazement through Denmark's **TIVOLI GARDENS**...

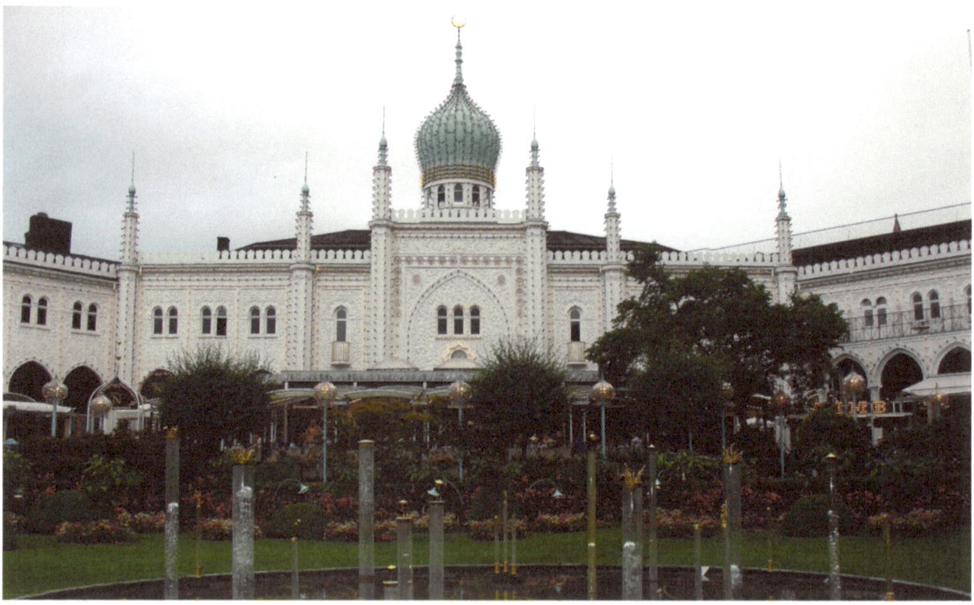

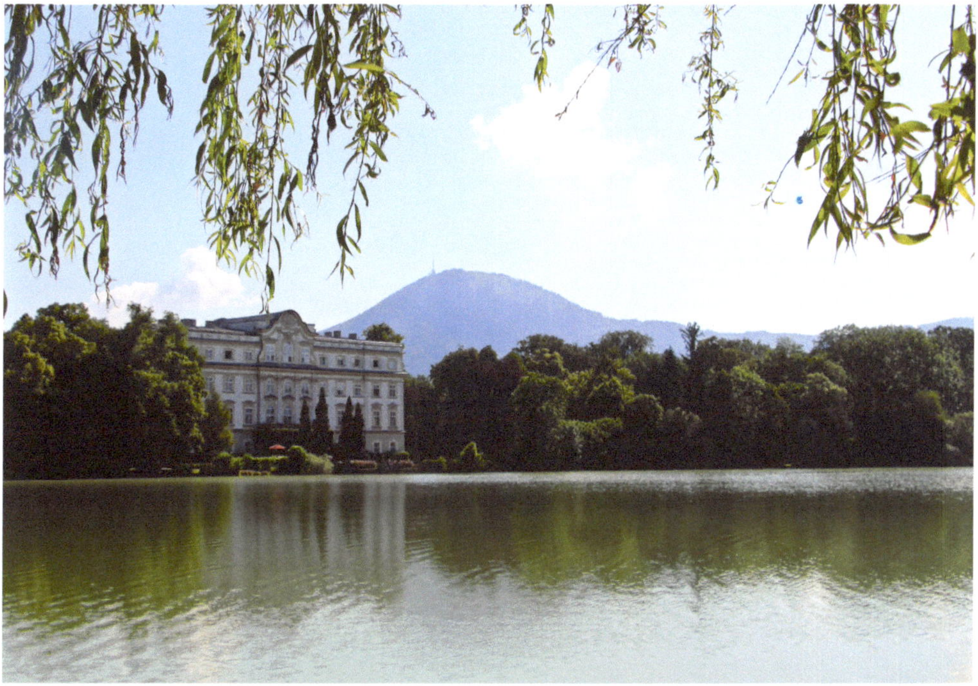

sang the familiar tunes of **THE SOUND OF MUSIC**
as we roamed the grounds of the **Von Trapp family** home in Austria...

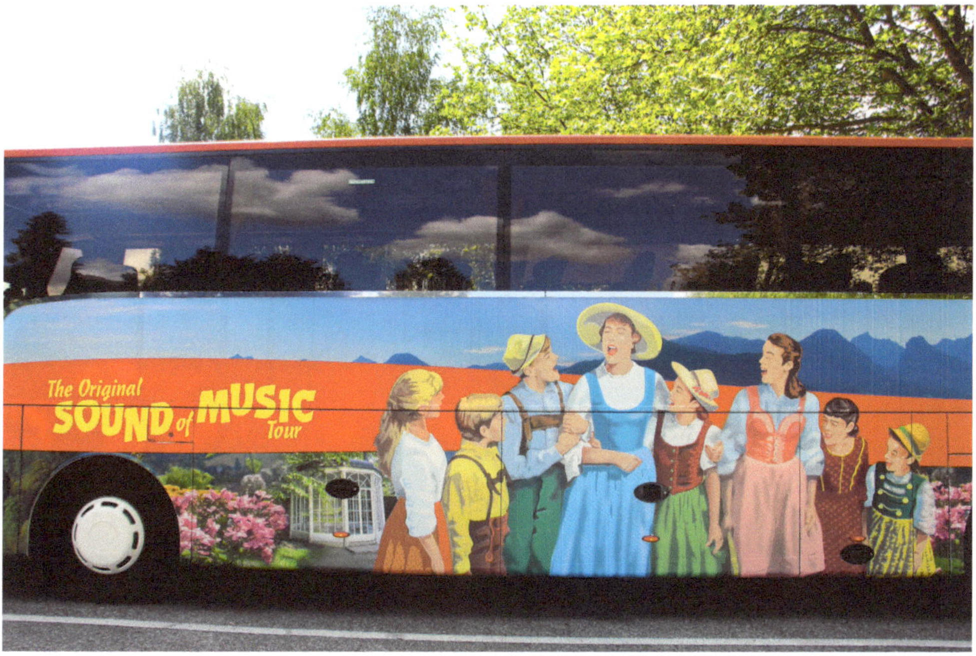

I enjoyed
the simplicity
of a cone of gelato
as we strolled past
the imposing

MONTE CARLO CASINO...

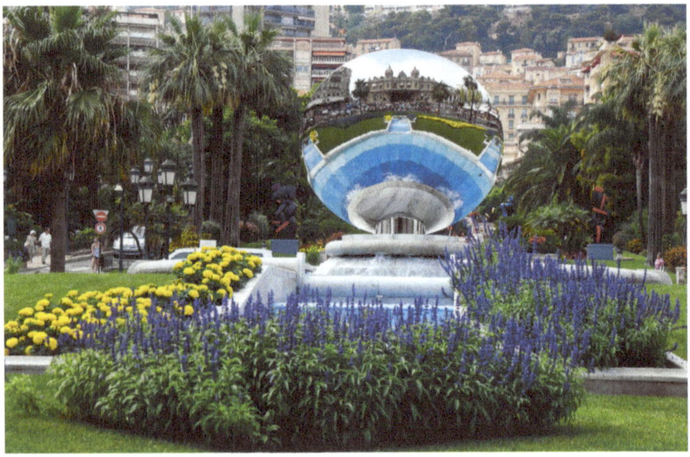

I and admired the
abundance of
yachts in that
vibrant

MEDITERRANEAN PORT...

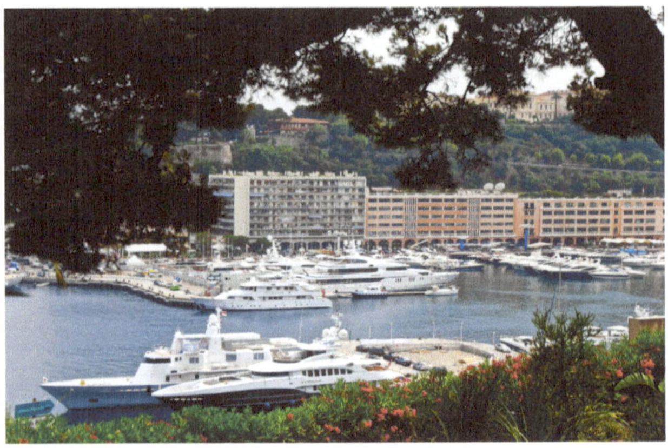

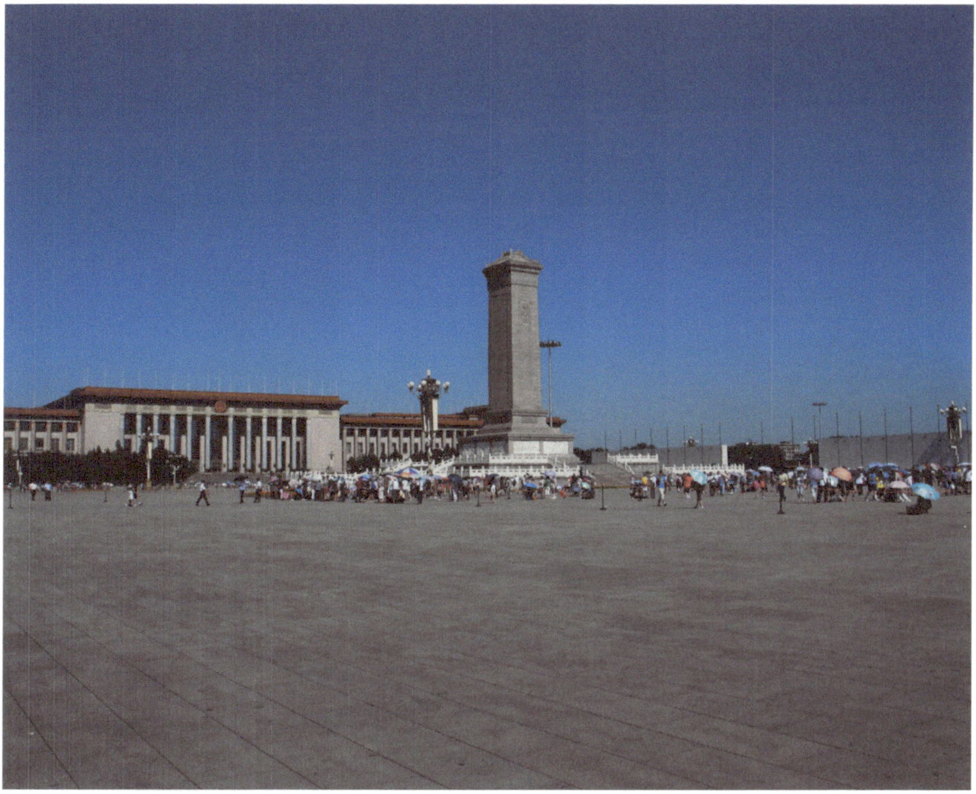

wandered history's pavement in

TIANANMEN SQUARE...

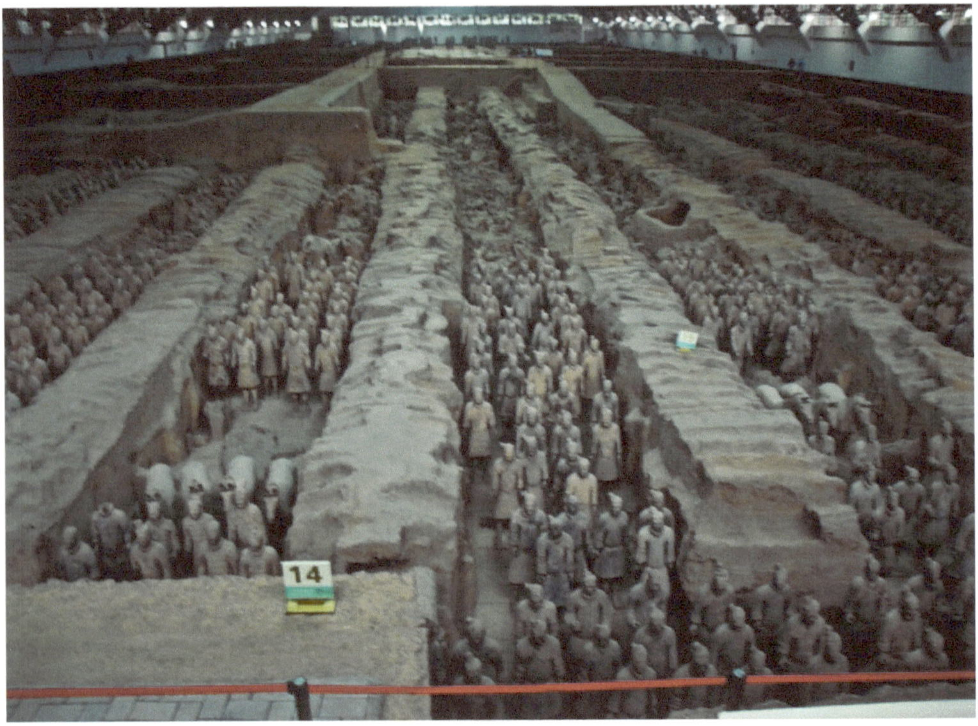

stood in awe
at the active dig site
of

XIAN'S TERRA COTTA WARRIORS...

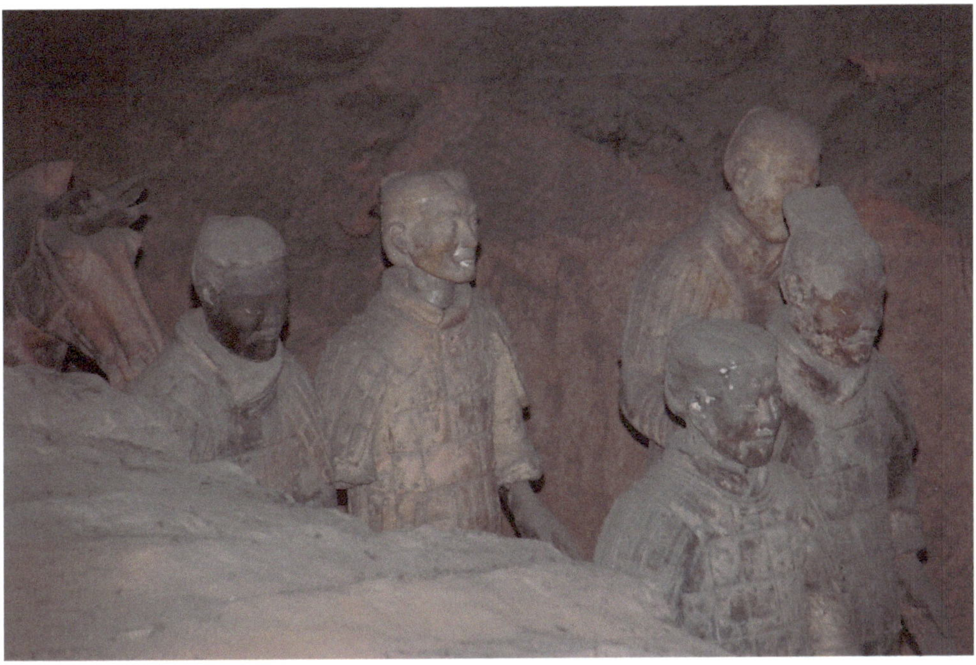

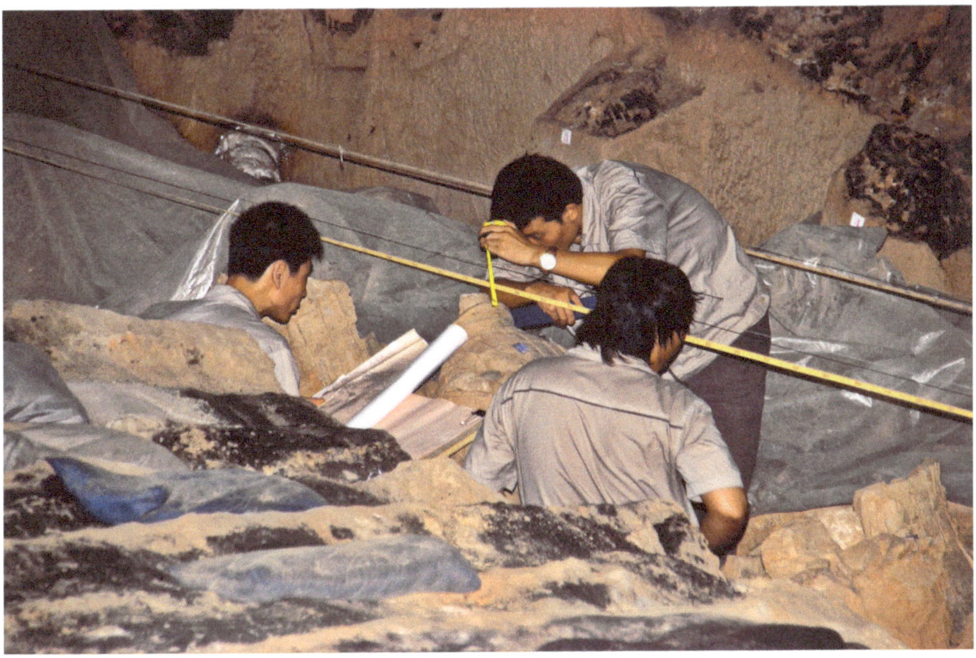

were astonished at the size and simplicity of Norway's

THOR HEYERDAHL'S KON TIKI...

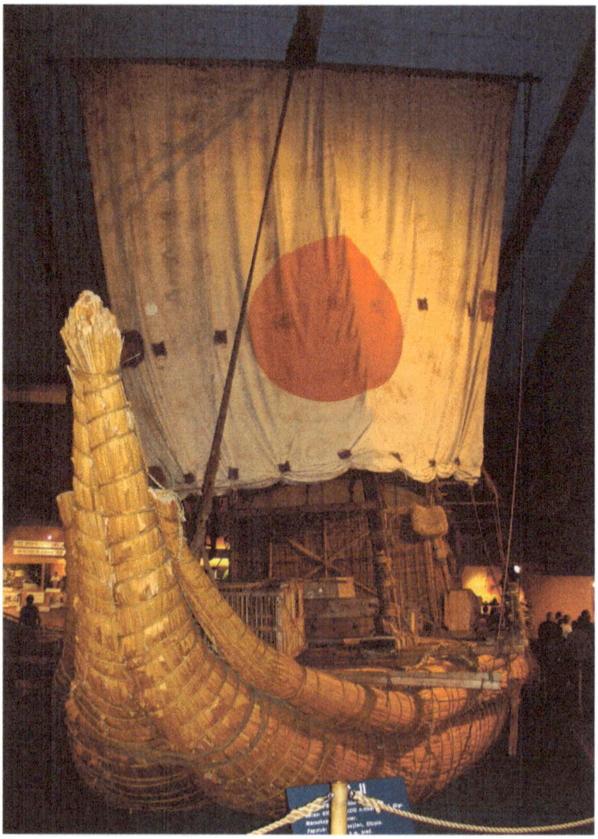

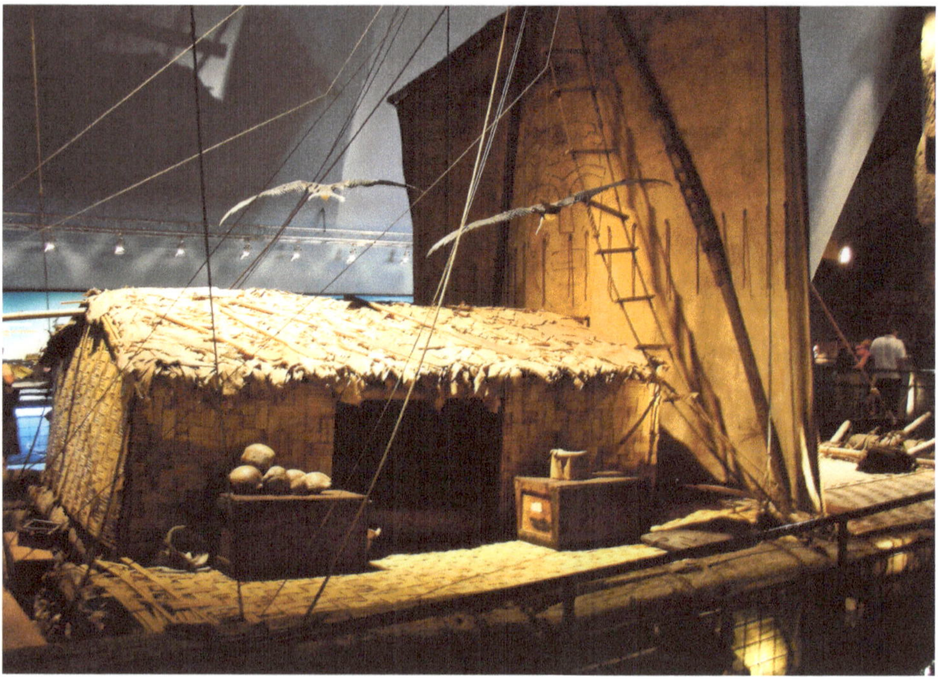

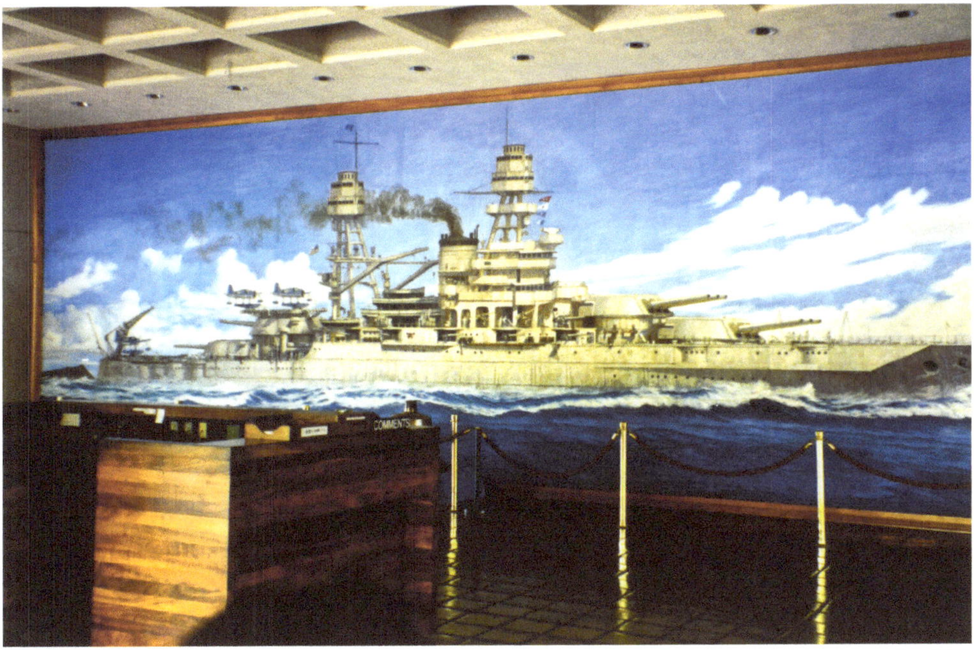

quitely reflected as we watched
the continuous oil leak from the sunken

WORLDWAR II BATTLESHIP USS ARIZONA

as it remains solemnly beneath Hawaii's waters...

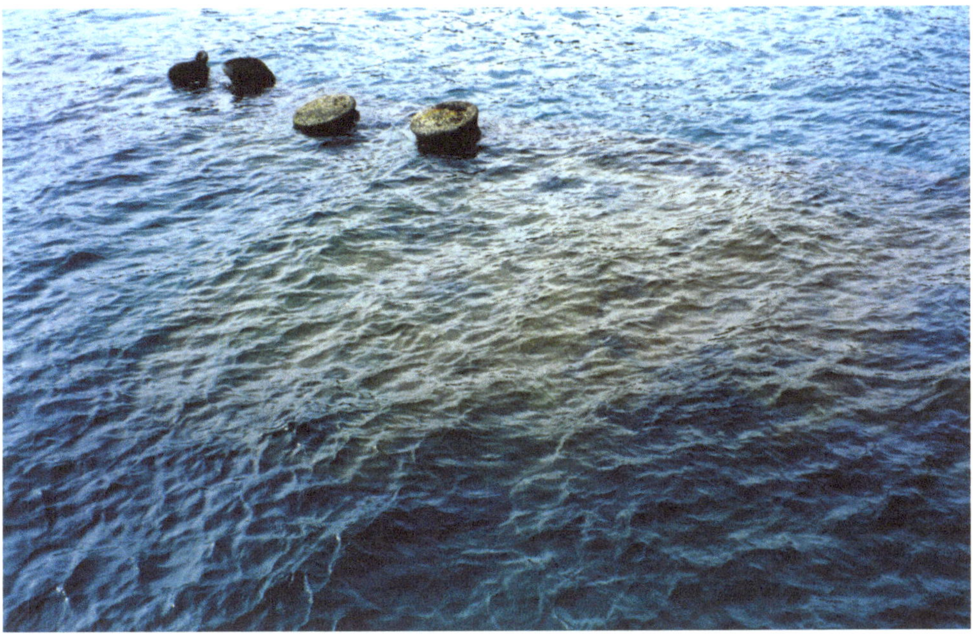

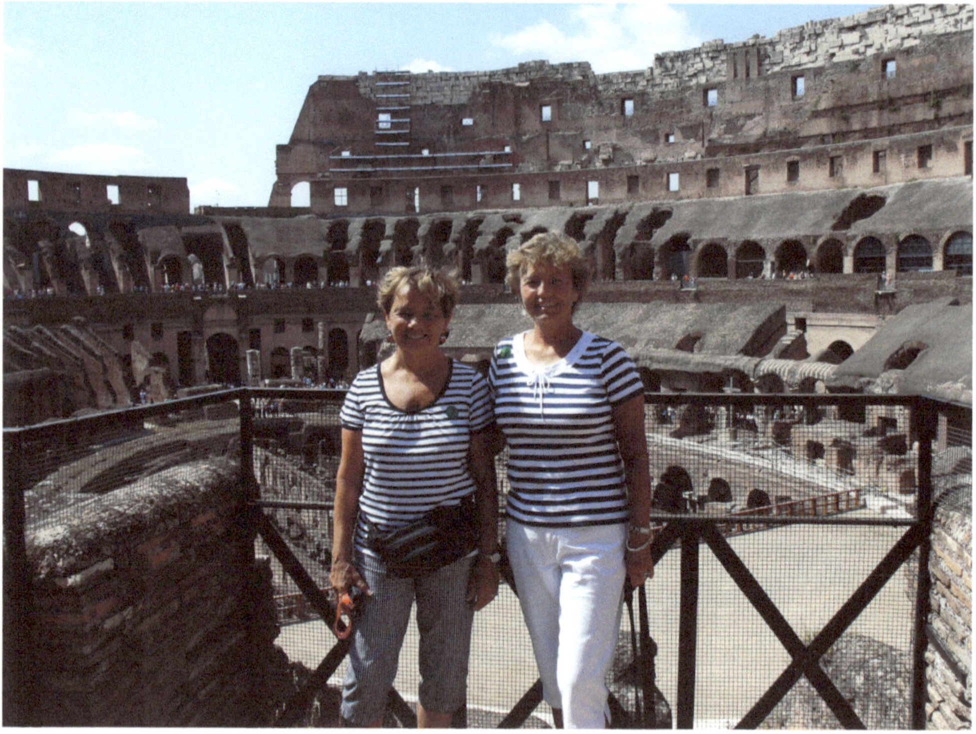

walked among the ancient ruins of

ROME'S COLOSSEUM...

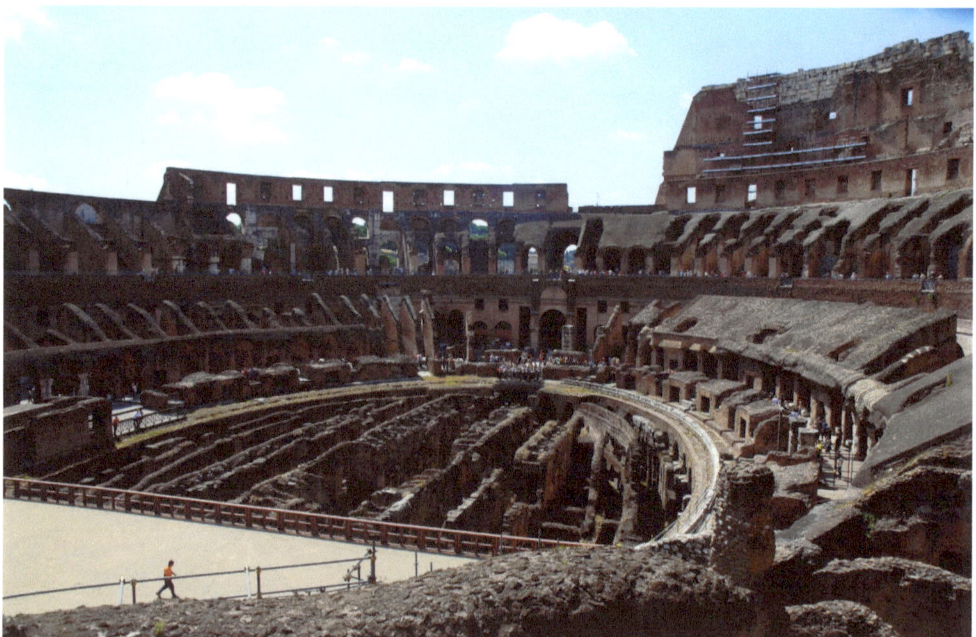

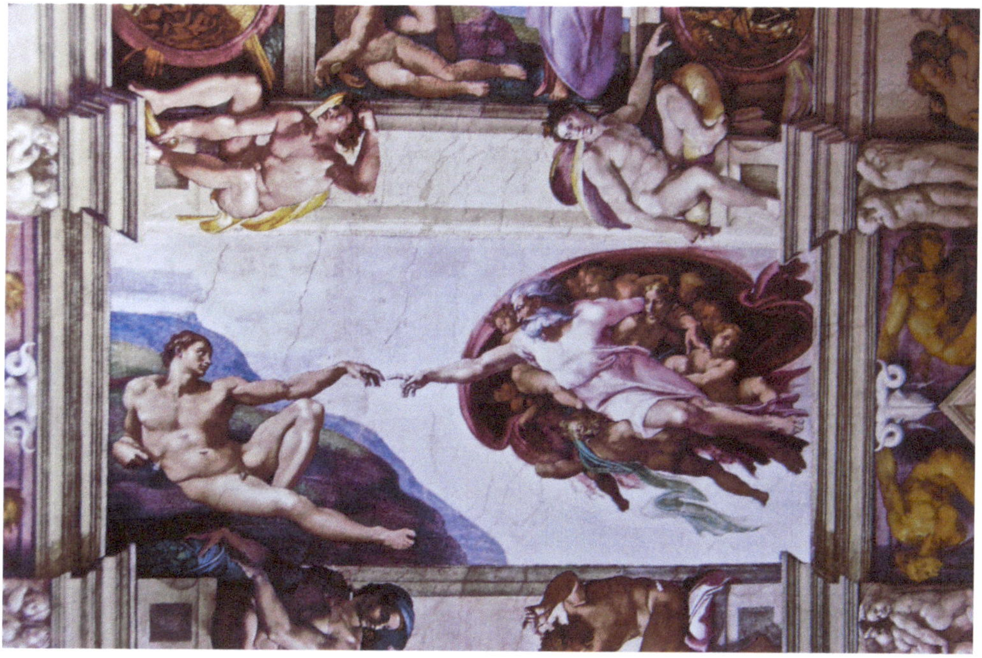

saw Michelangelo's masterpiece in the

VATICAN'S SISTINE CHAPEL...

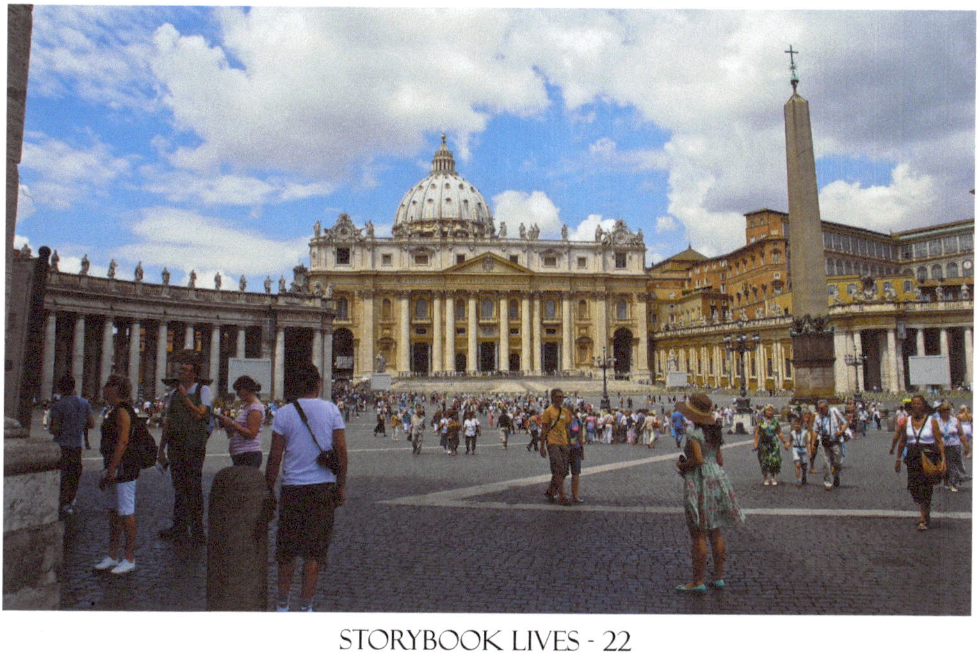

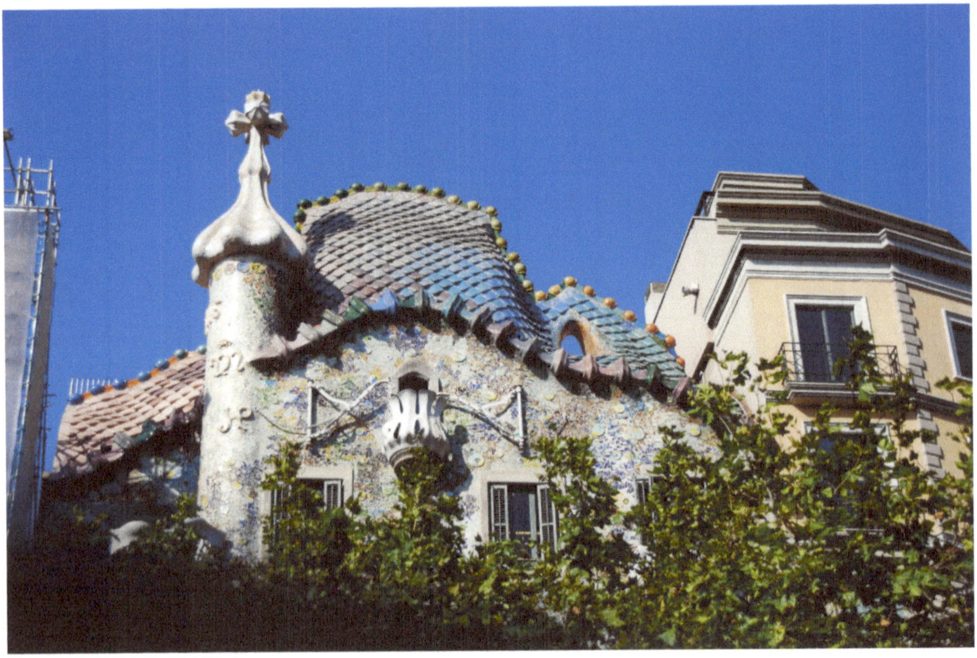

I came face to face with the glitziness of
BARCELONA'S GAUDI...

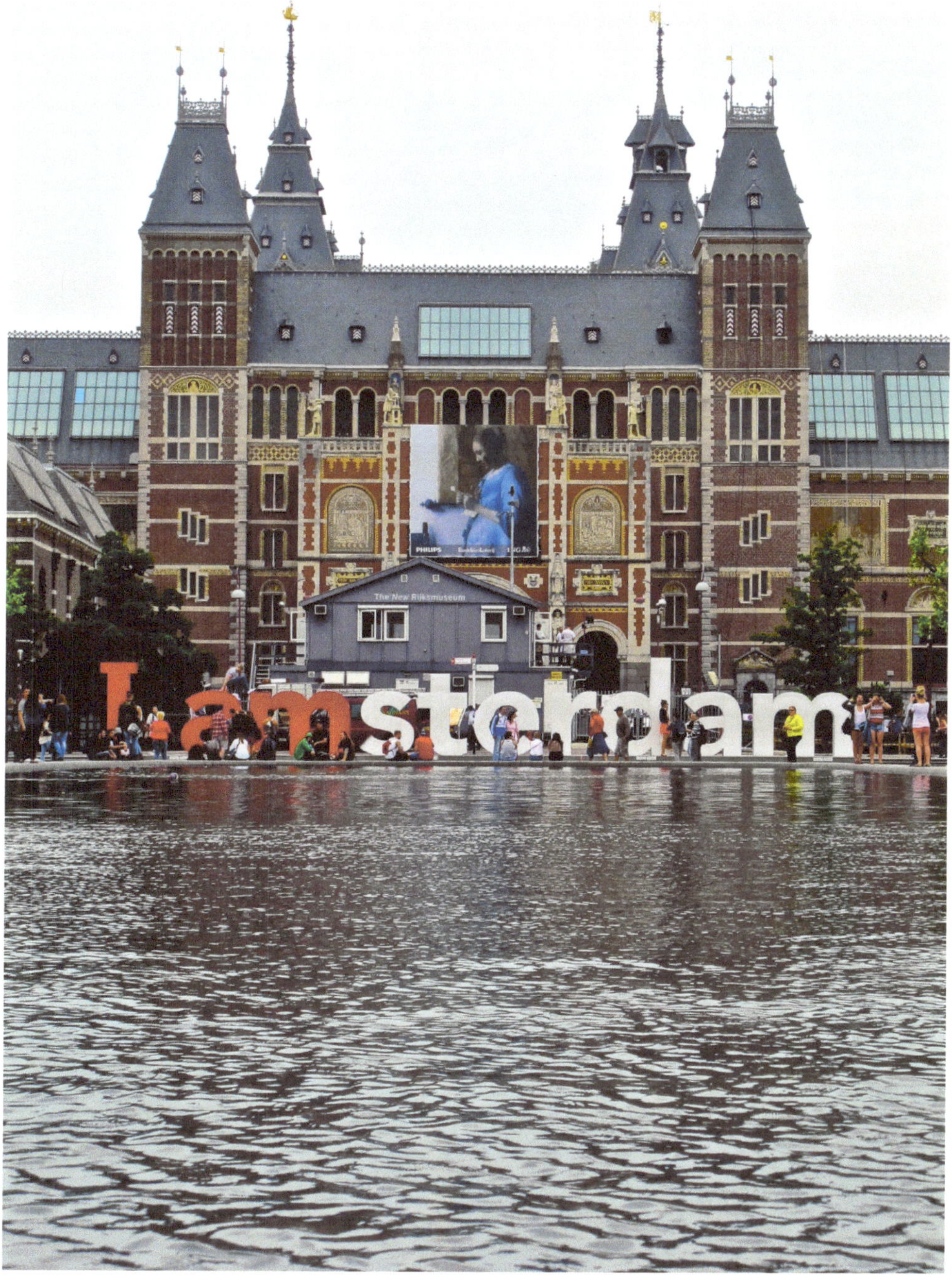

and the stirring life and art of
VAN GOGH in **AMSTERDAM... I**

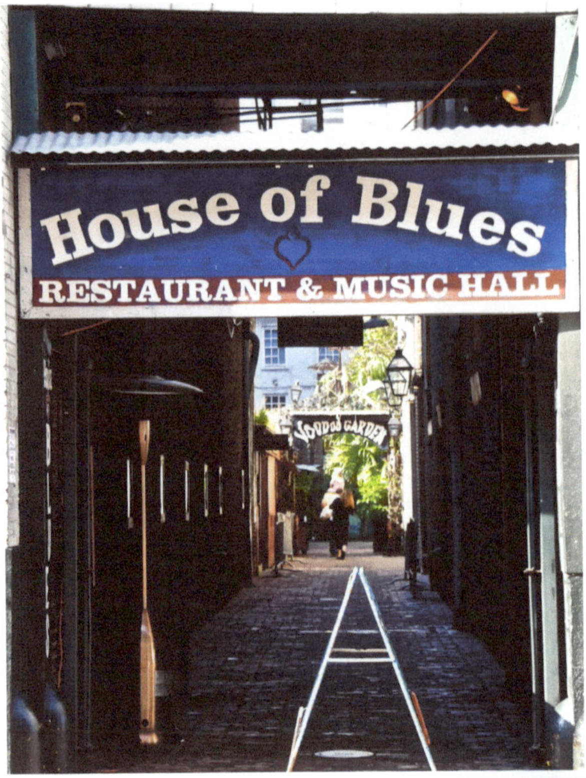

stood entranced by
Etta James
singing her classic

"AT LAST"

in the

NEW ORLEANS HOUSE OF BLUES...

attended an open
jazz festival
in the seaside
town of

NICE, FRANCE...

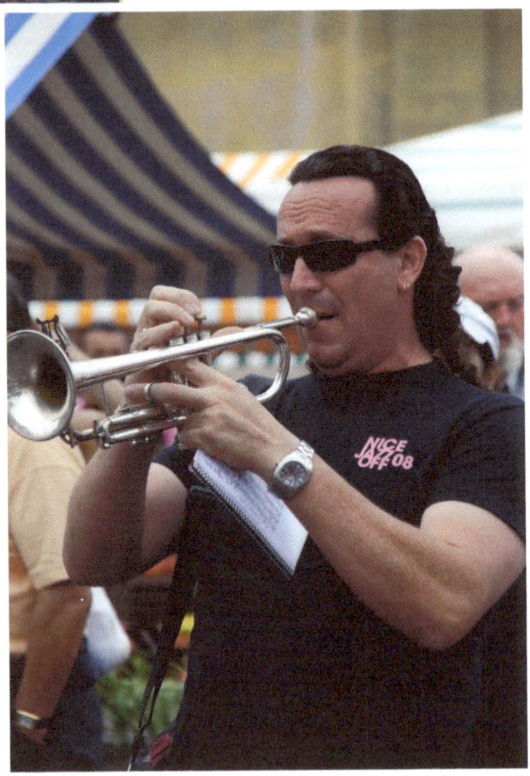

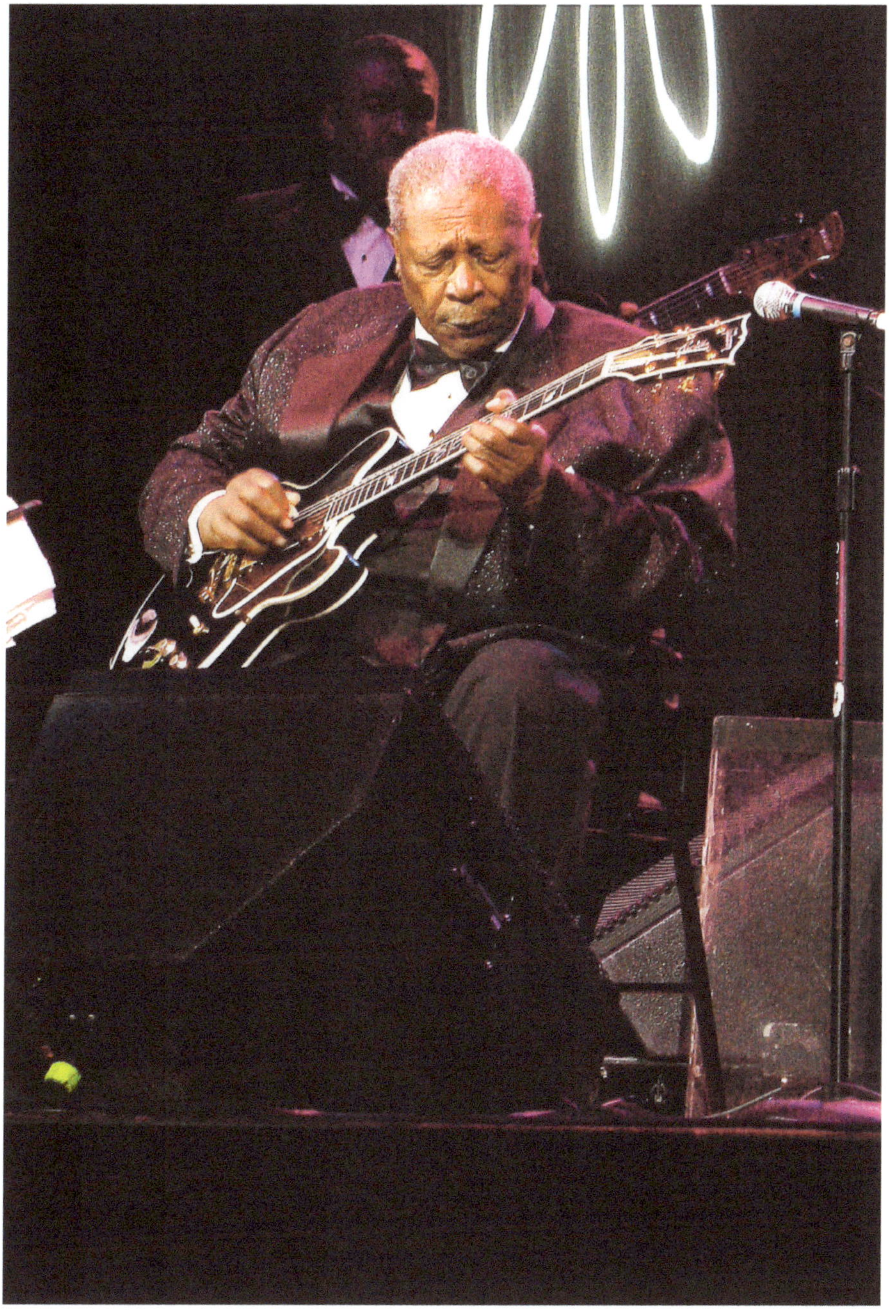

I secured front row seats to celebrate
B.B. KING'S birthday in Biloxi...

rode and
bathed
elephants in

THAILAND...

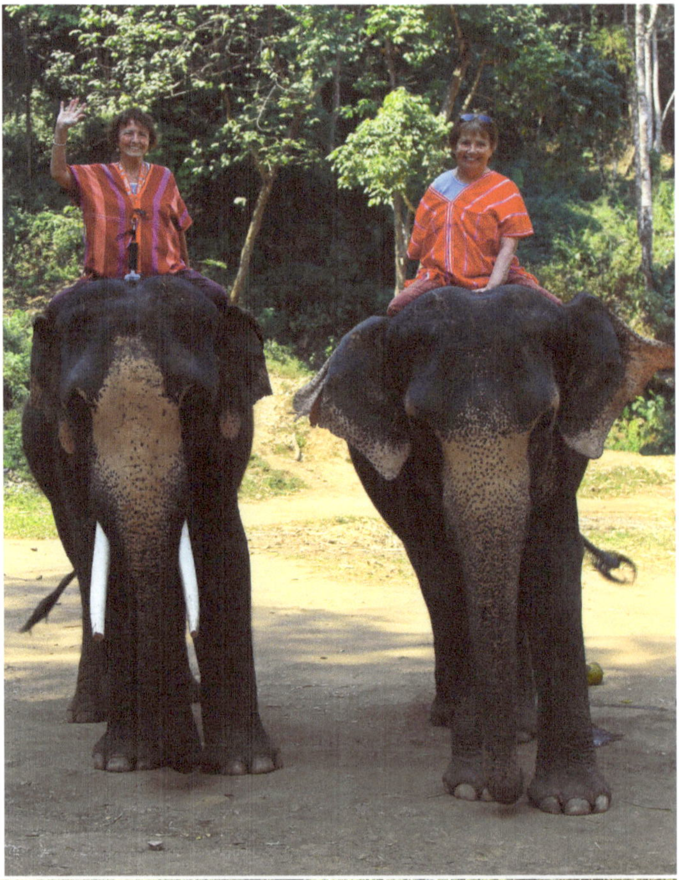

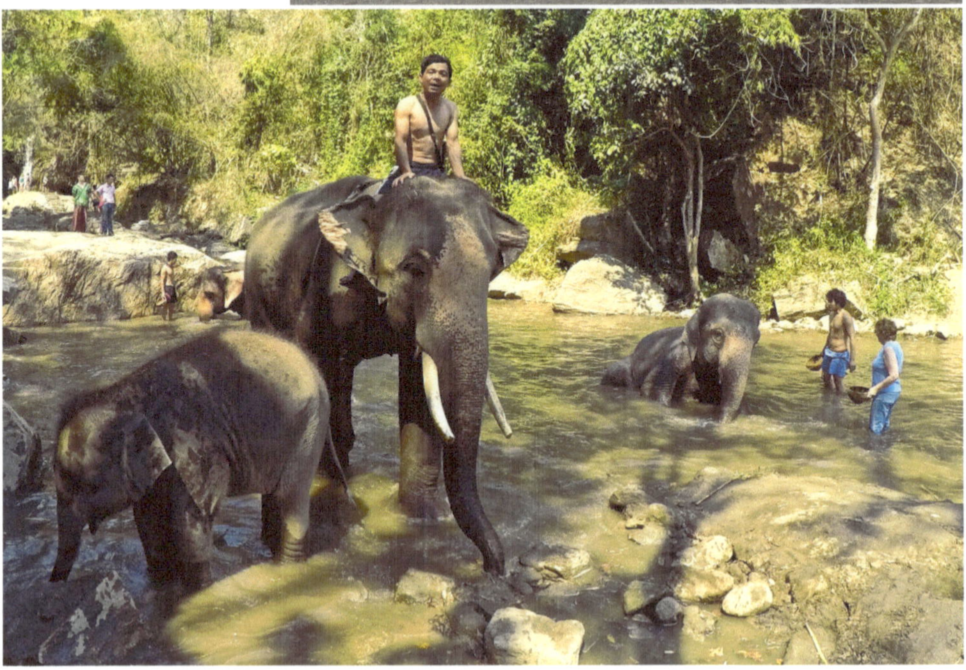

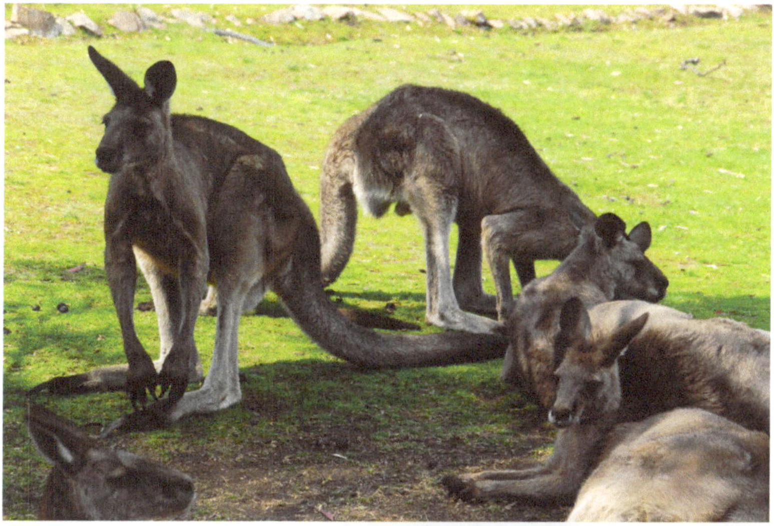

eagerly played
with kangaroos
and koalas in
AUSTRALIA...

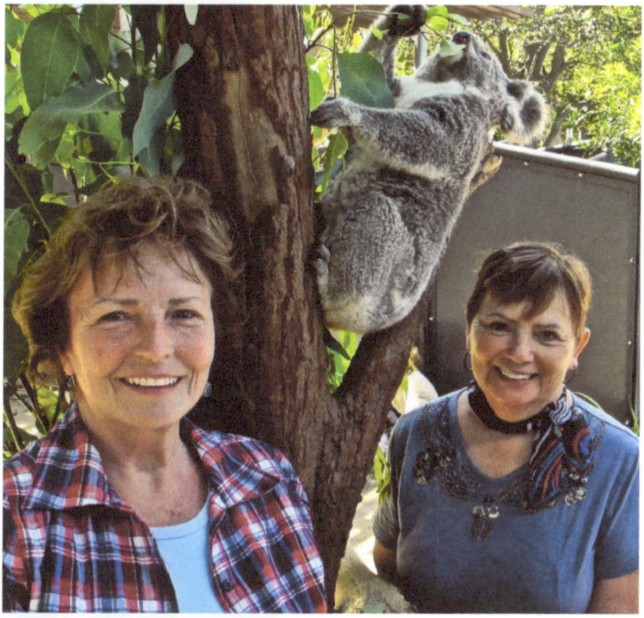

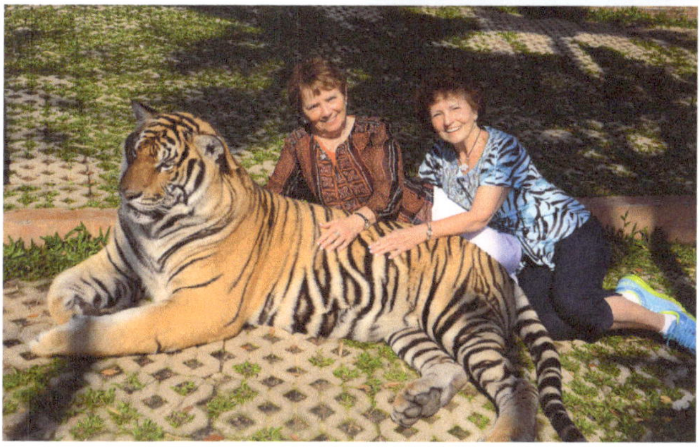

and cautiously
interacted with
BENGAL
TIGERS in
SOUTHEAST
ASIA

swam with
stingrays in
GRAND CAYMAN'S
warm waters...

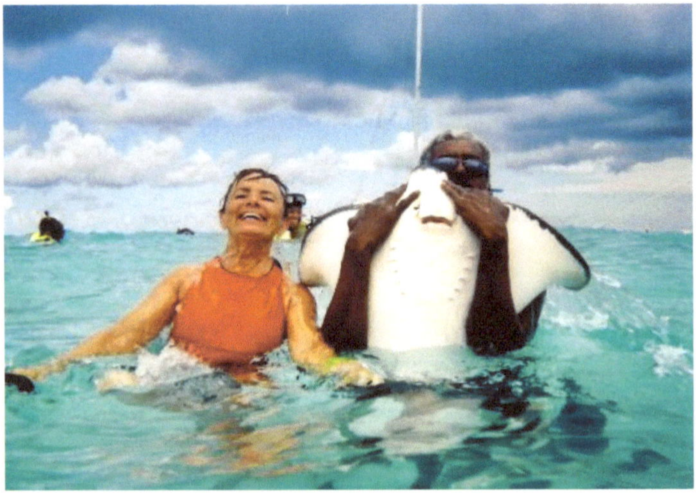

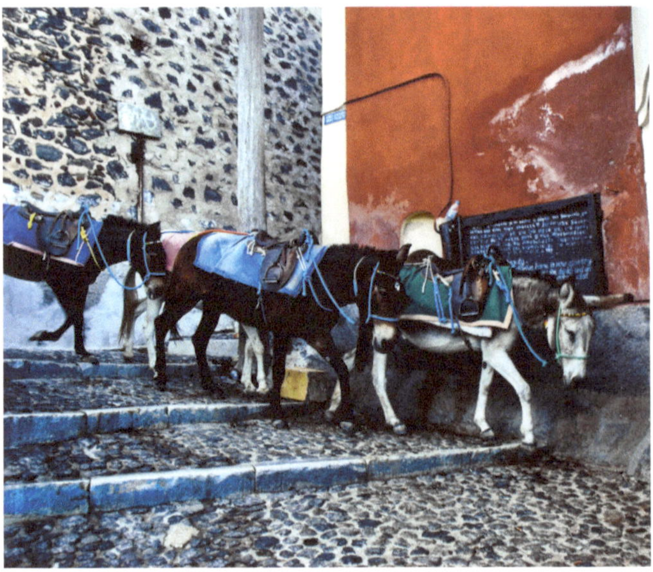

rode donkeys to
SANTORINI'S
lofty blue and
white city...

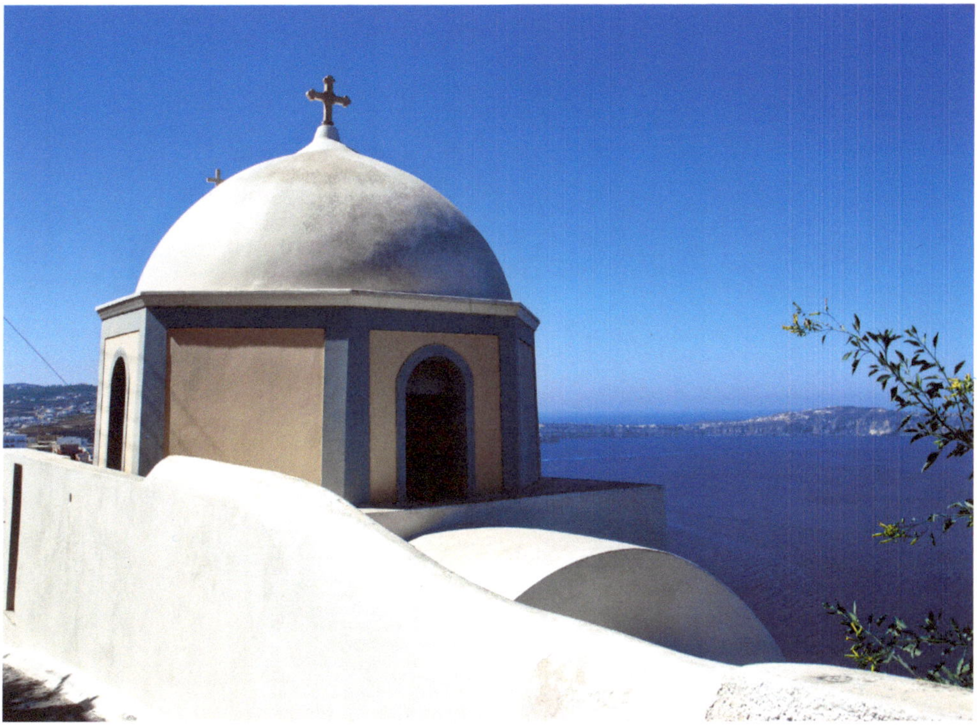

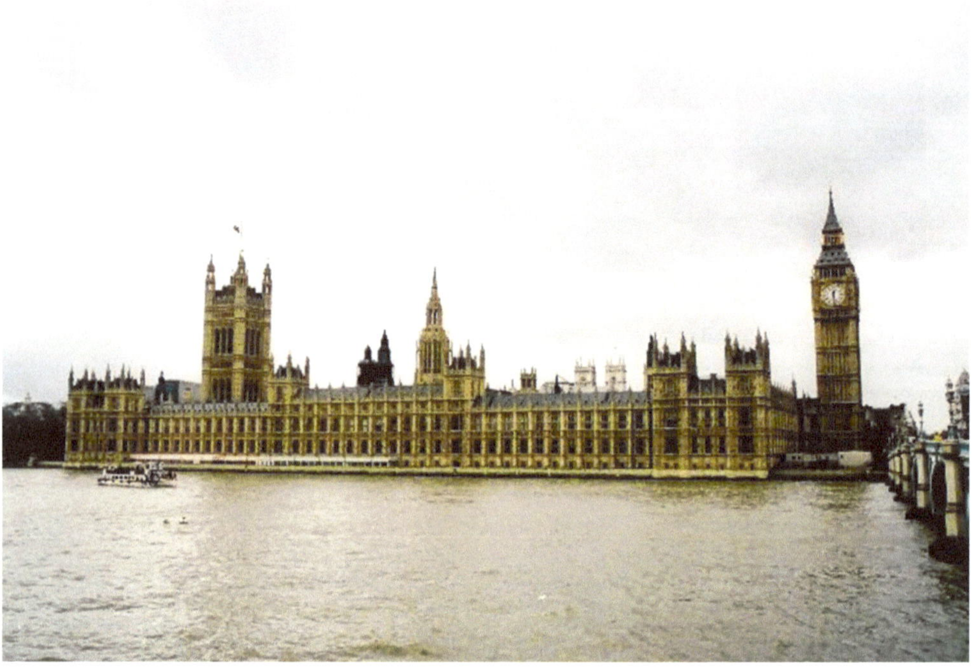

I set our watches by **BIG BEN** in **LONDON**, the city
in whichWilliam Shakespeare was establised as a man of theater...

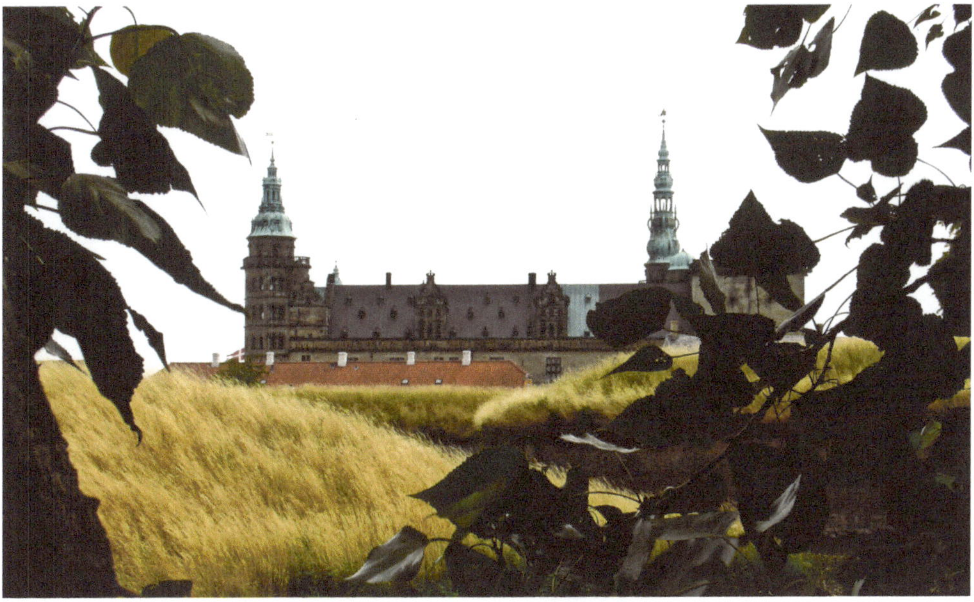

I toured **HAMLET'S CASTLE** in Denmark...

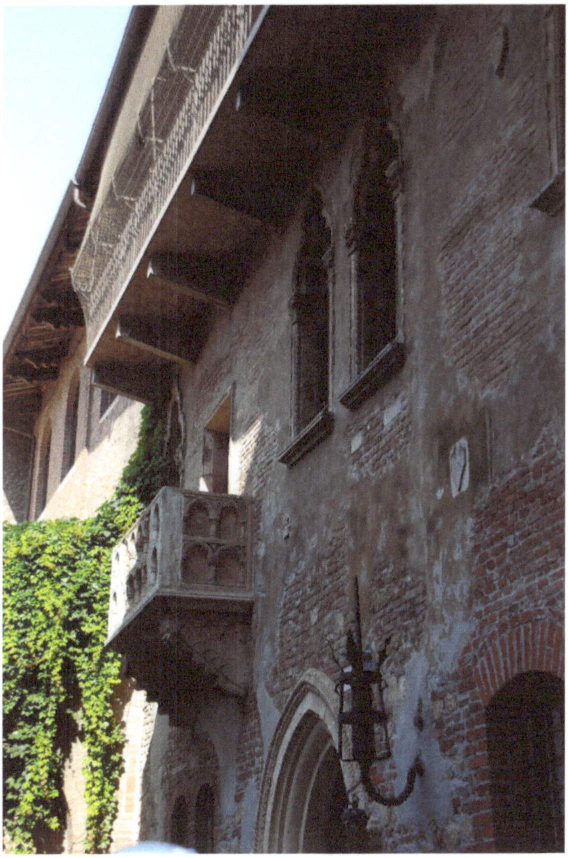

and

JULIET'S

BALCONY

inVerona, Italy...

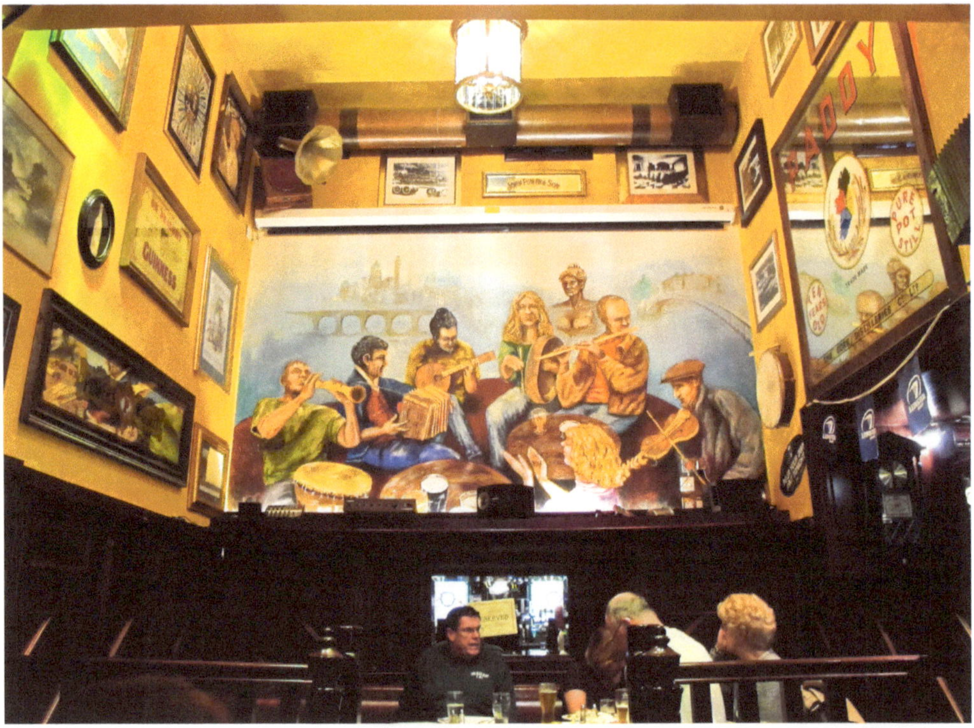

took part in a
PUB CRAWL
LITERARY
TOUR
in **DUBLIN,**
IRELAND...

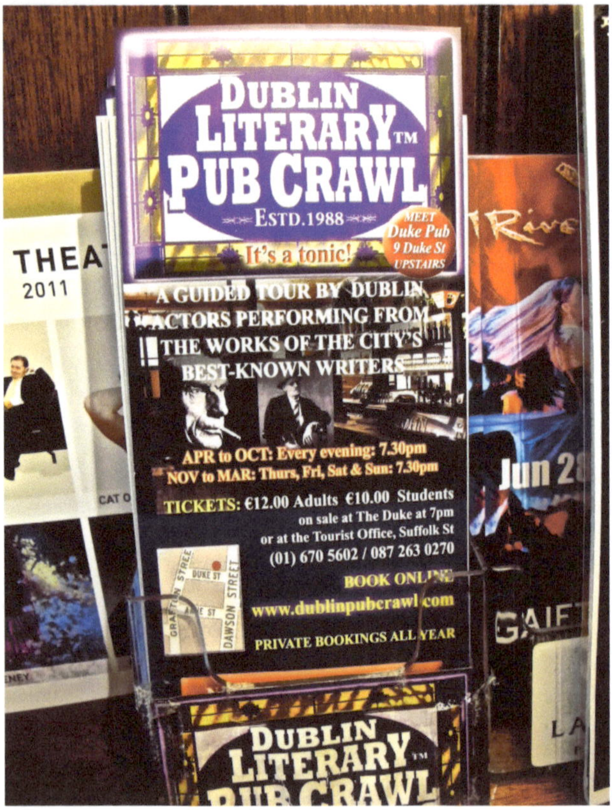

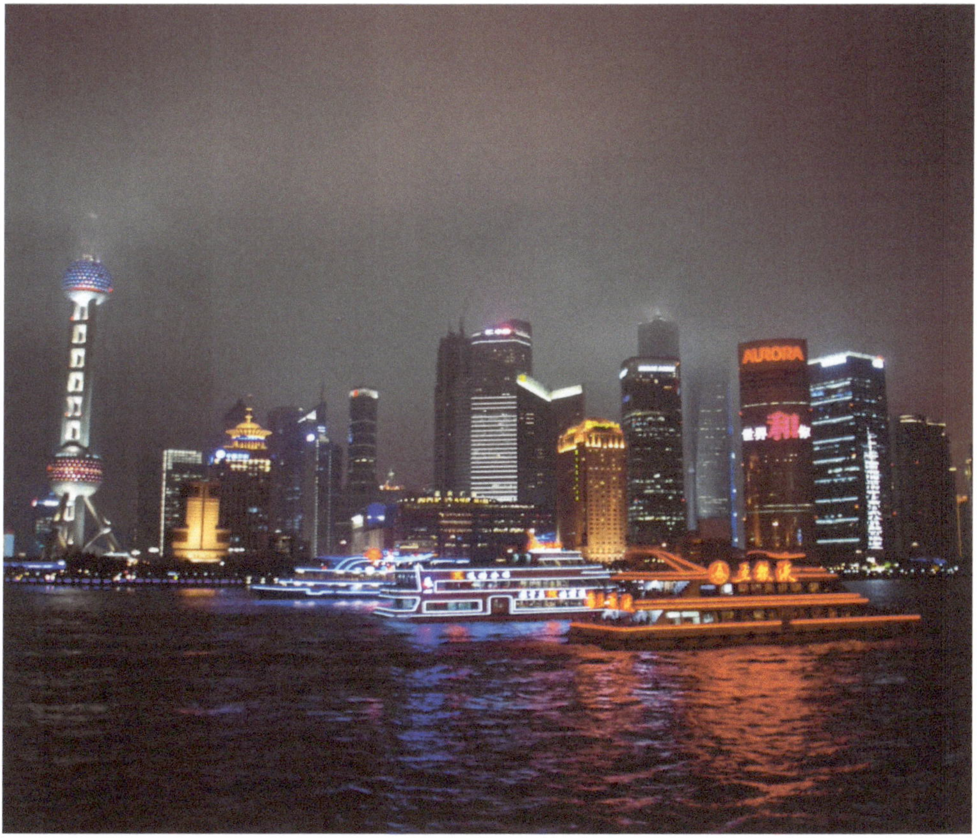

I strolled through the amusement park-like atmosphere of **SHANGHAI'S BUND**...

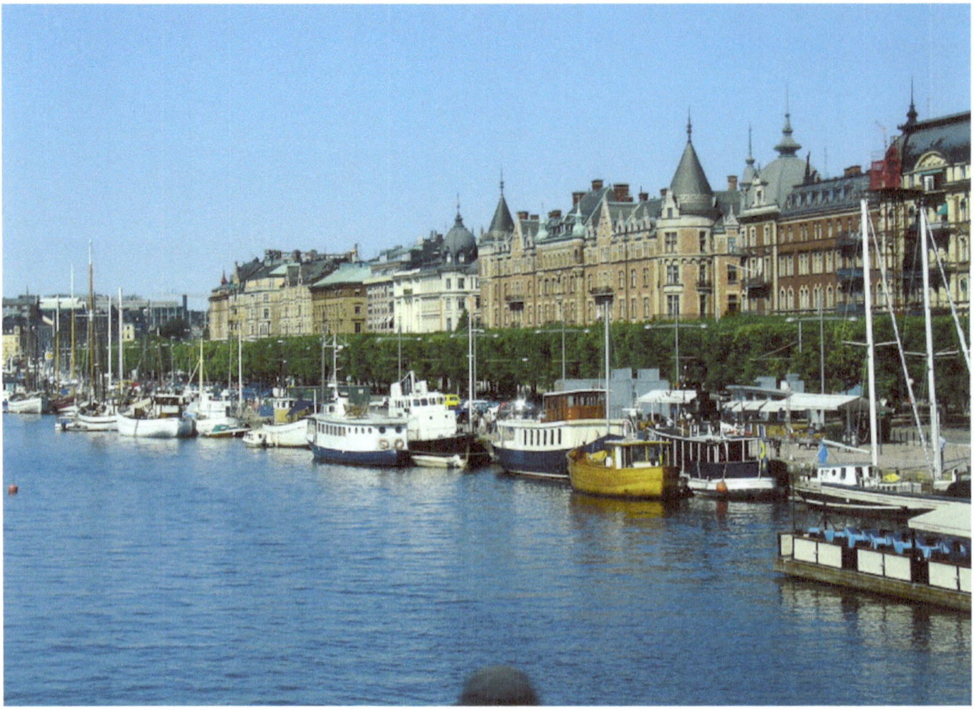

I watched as the

SWEDISH ROYAL GUARD

paraded through the streets of Stockholm...

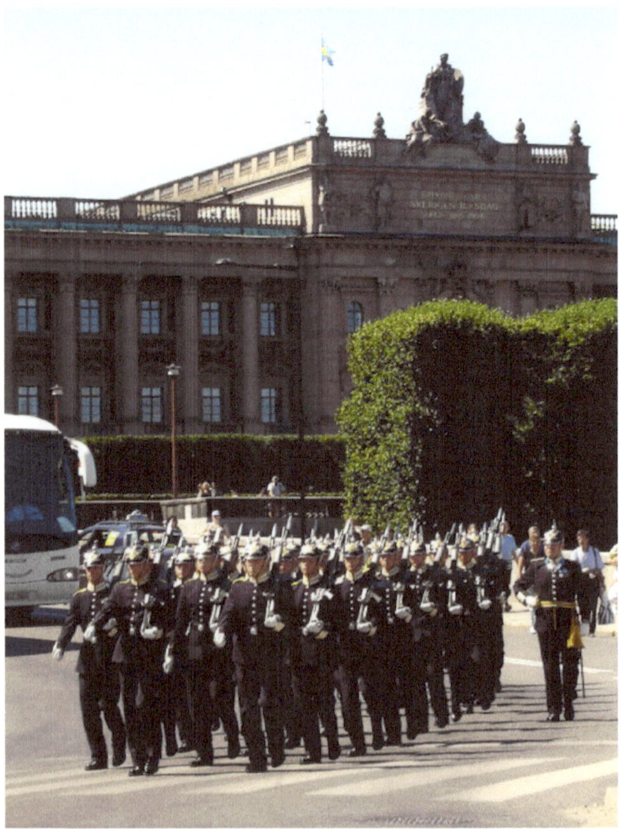

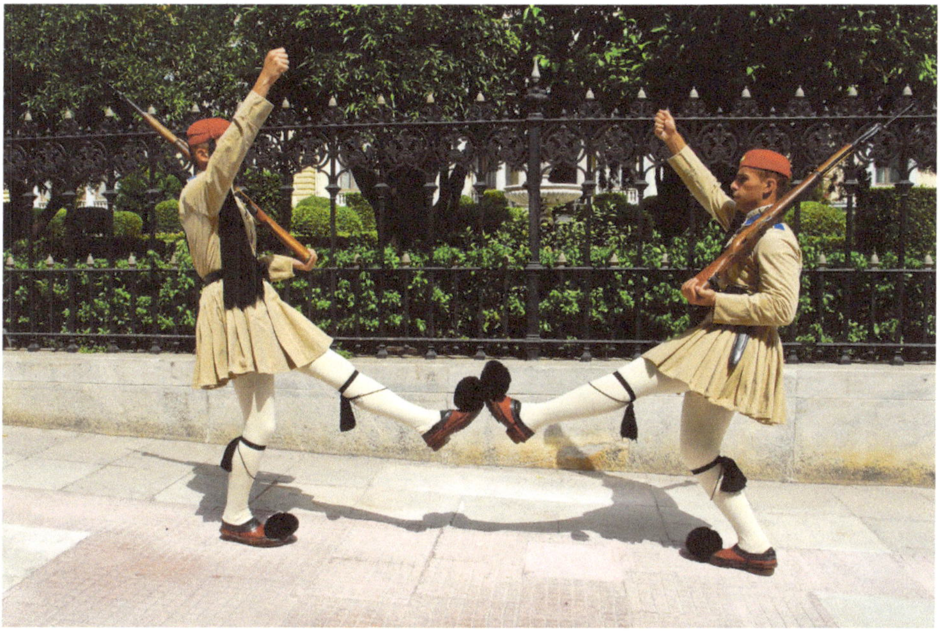

I saw the changing of the **PRESIDENTIAL GUARD** in Athens

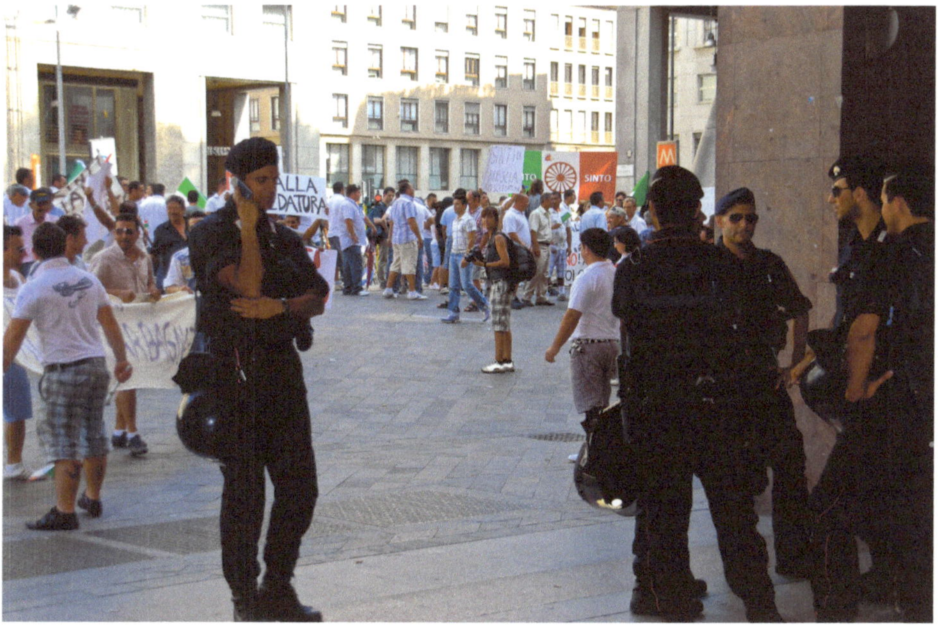

and observed the **MILAN POLICE** standing by,
preparing for a protest march... I

safaried in

KENYA...

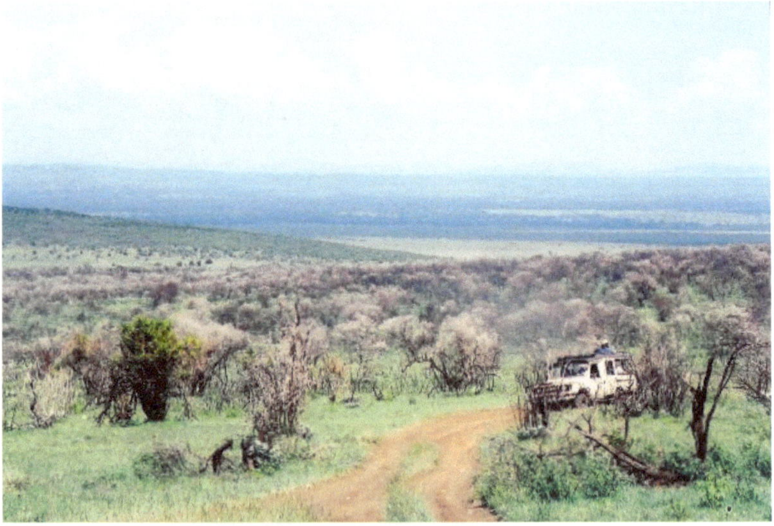

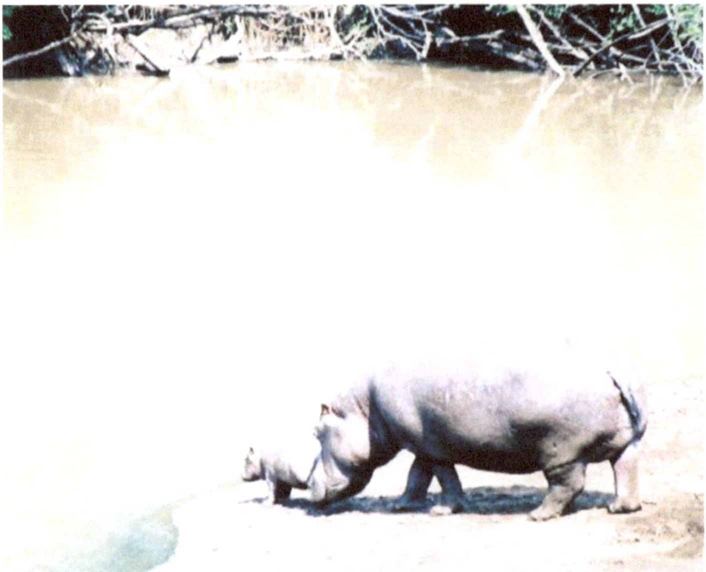

watched as a

NEWBORN HIPPO

took its first steps to the river...

saw a

MOTHER CHEETAH

teaching her cub to hunt...

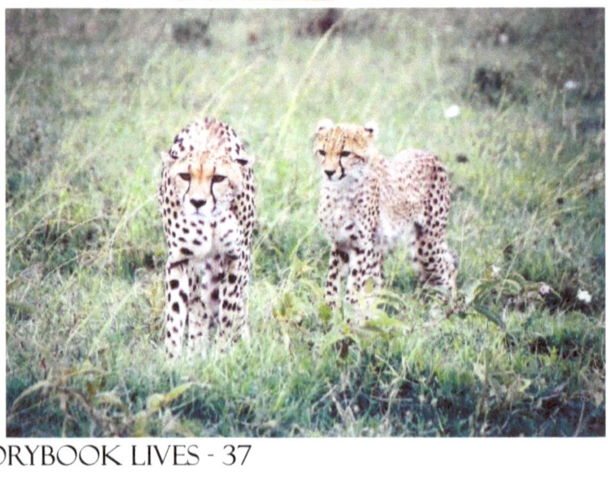

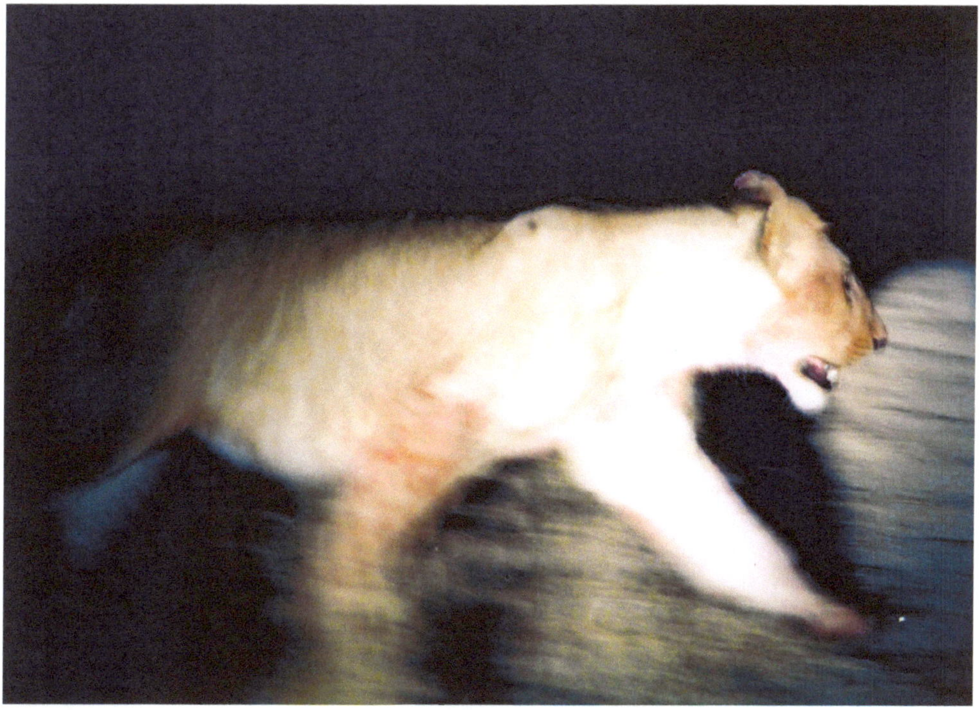

I watched **LIONS** at night fighting over a kill...

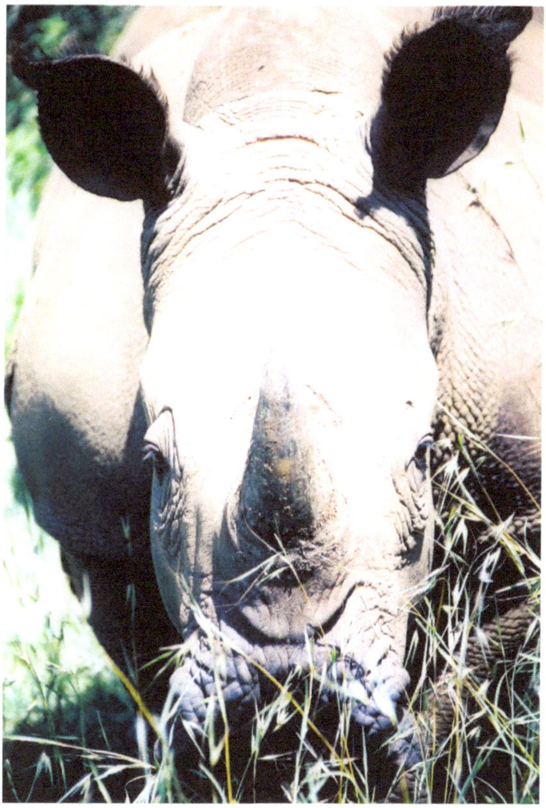

I faced a **WILD RHINO** in the open Serengeti...

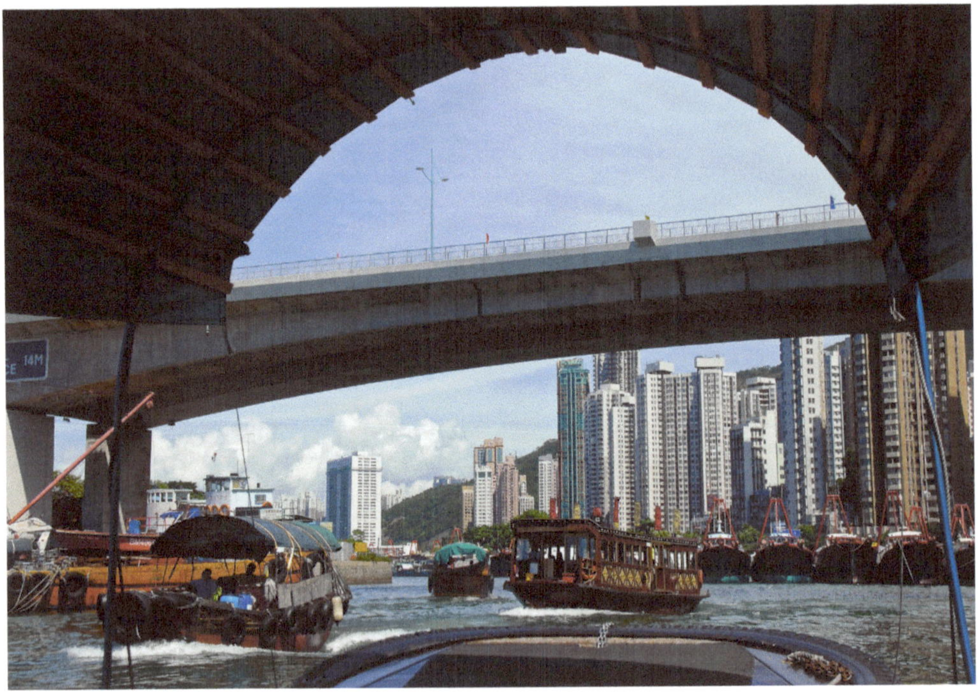

took a junk across **HONG KONG'S** harbor...

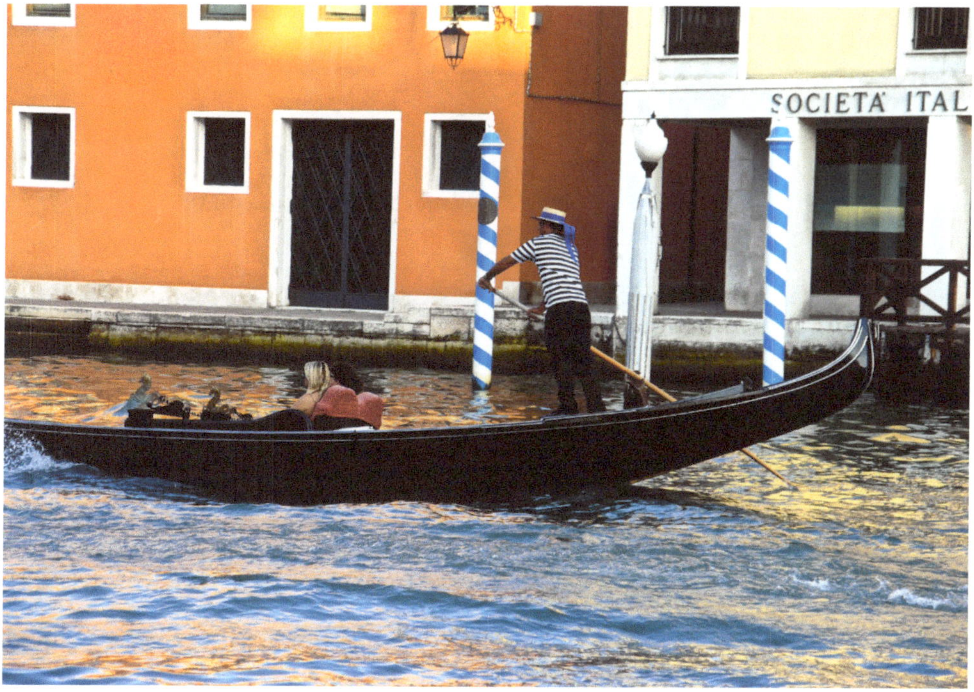

and a gondola through the

CANALS OF VENICE...

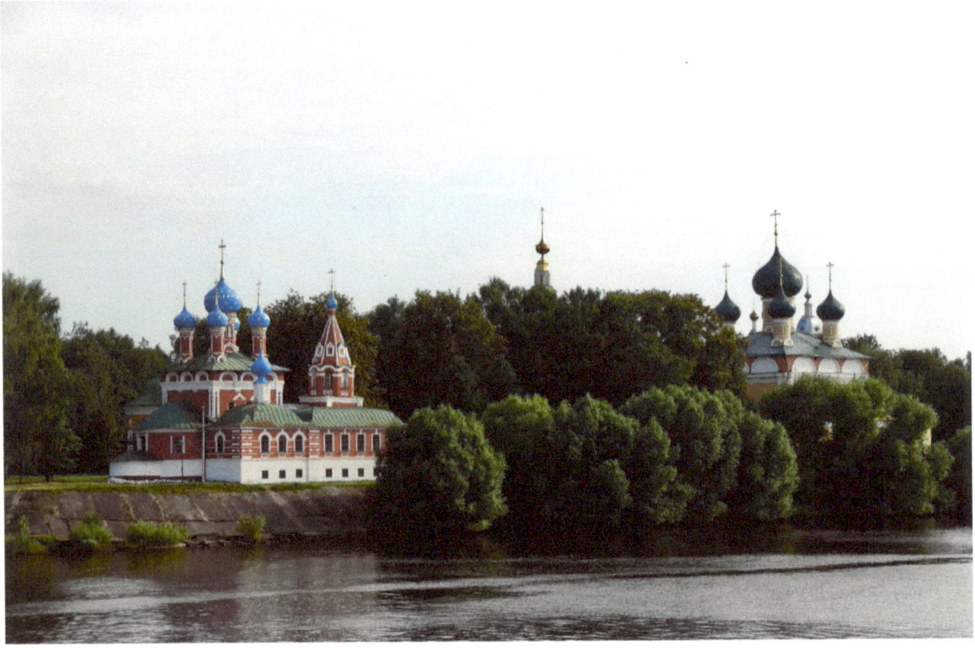

sailed the waterway of the **RUSSIAN CZARS**...

from **MOSCOW**...

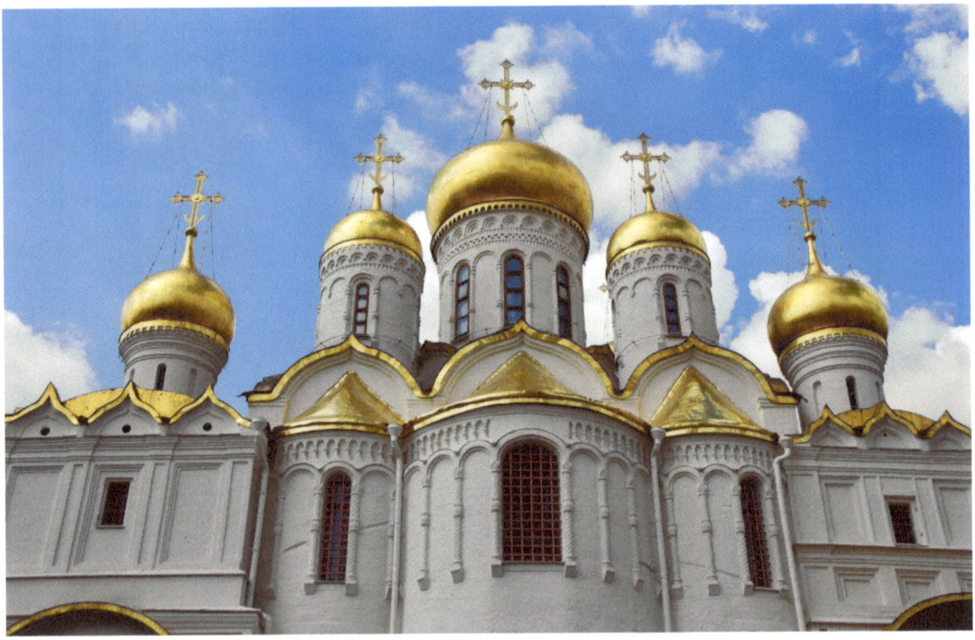

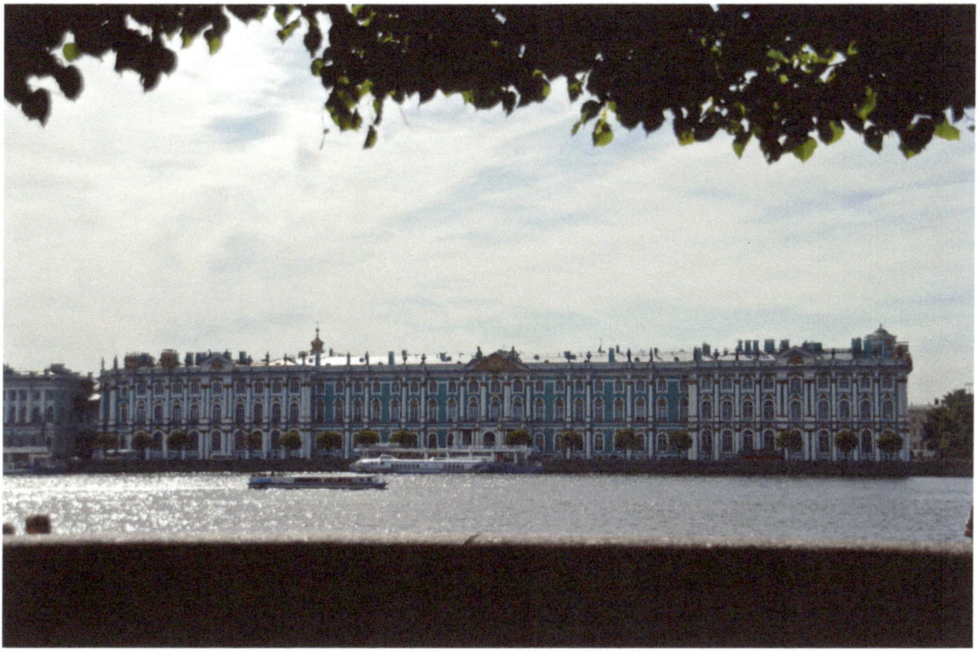

to **ST. PETERSBURG...**

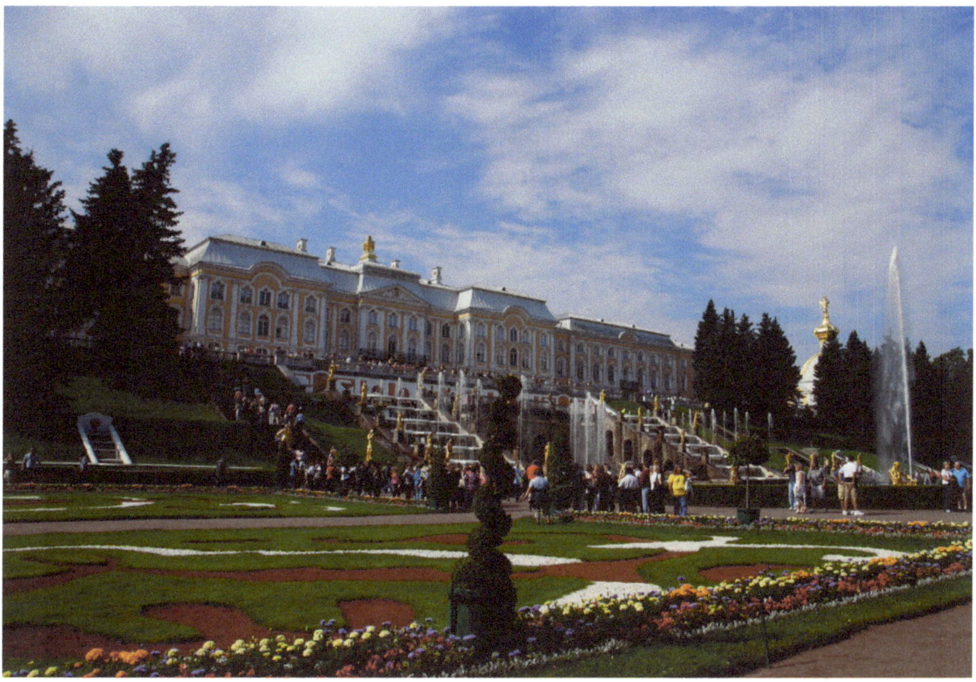

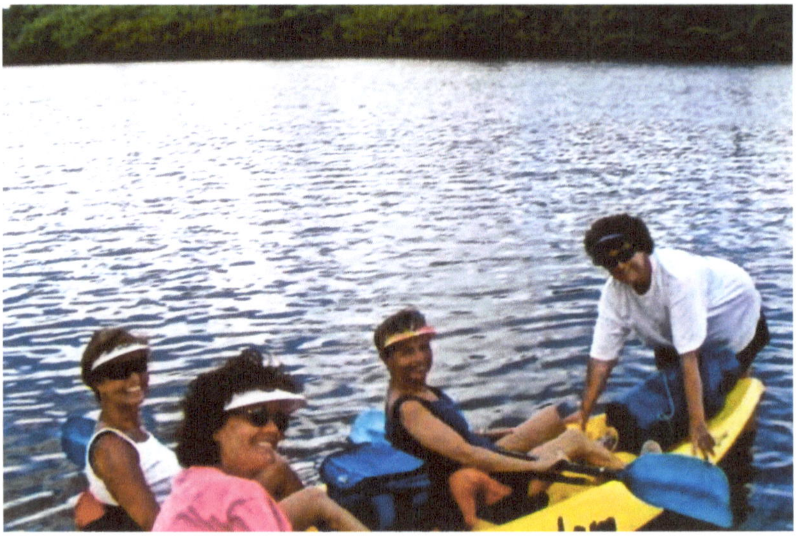

I kayaked **HAWAII'S** calm waters...
braved the **SNOWY TETONS** in dogsleds...
and rafted the rushing white waters of **COSTA RICA**...

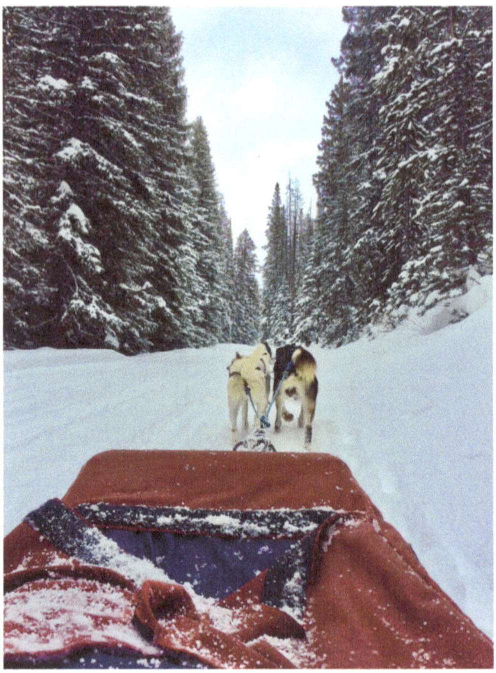

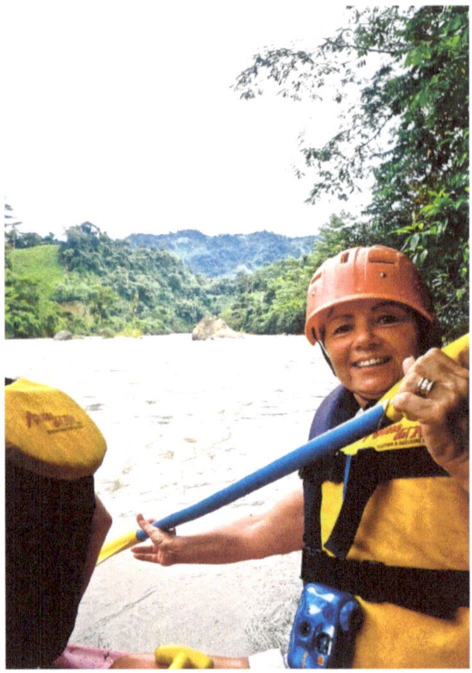

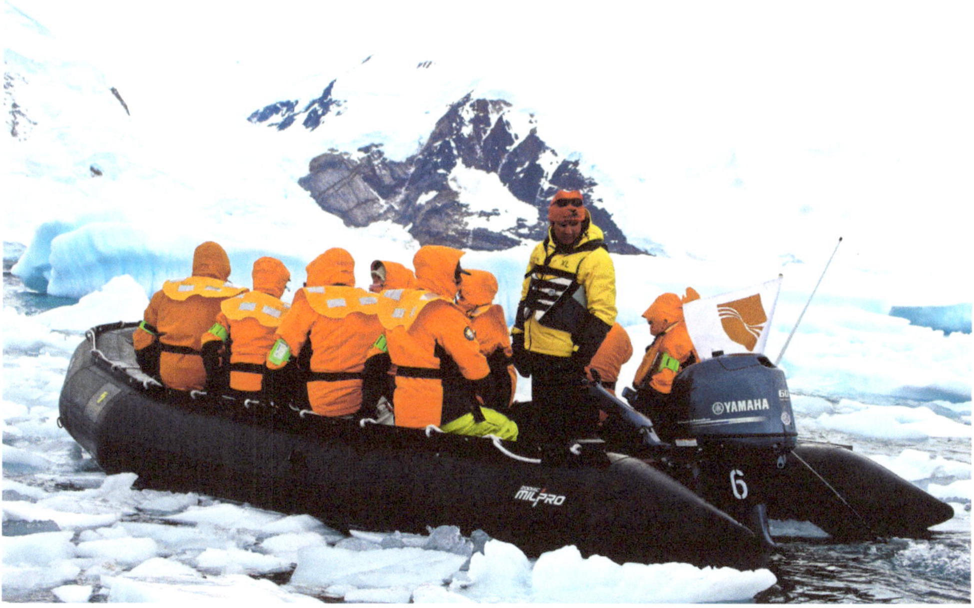

I took a **ZODIAC** to **ANTARCTICA'S** icy continent...

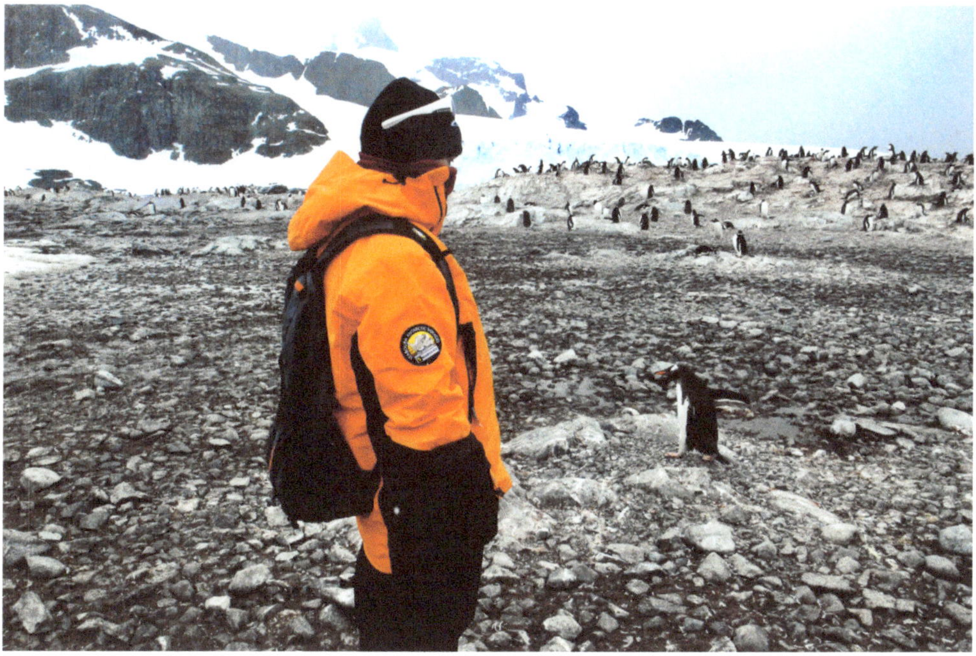

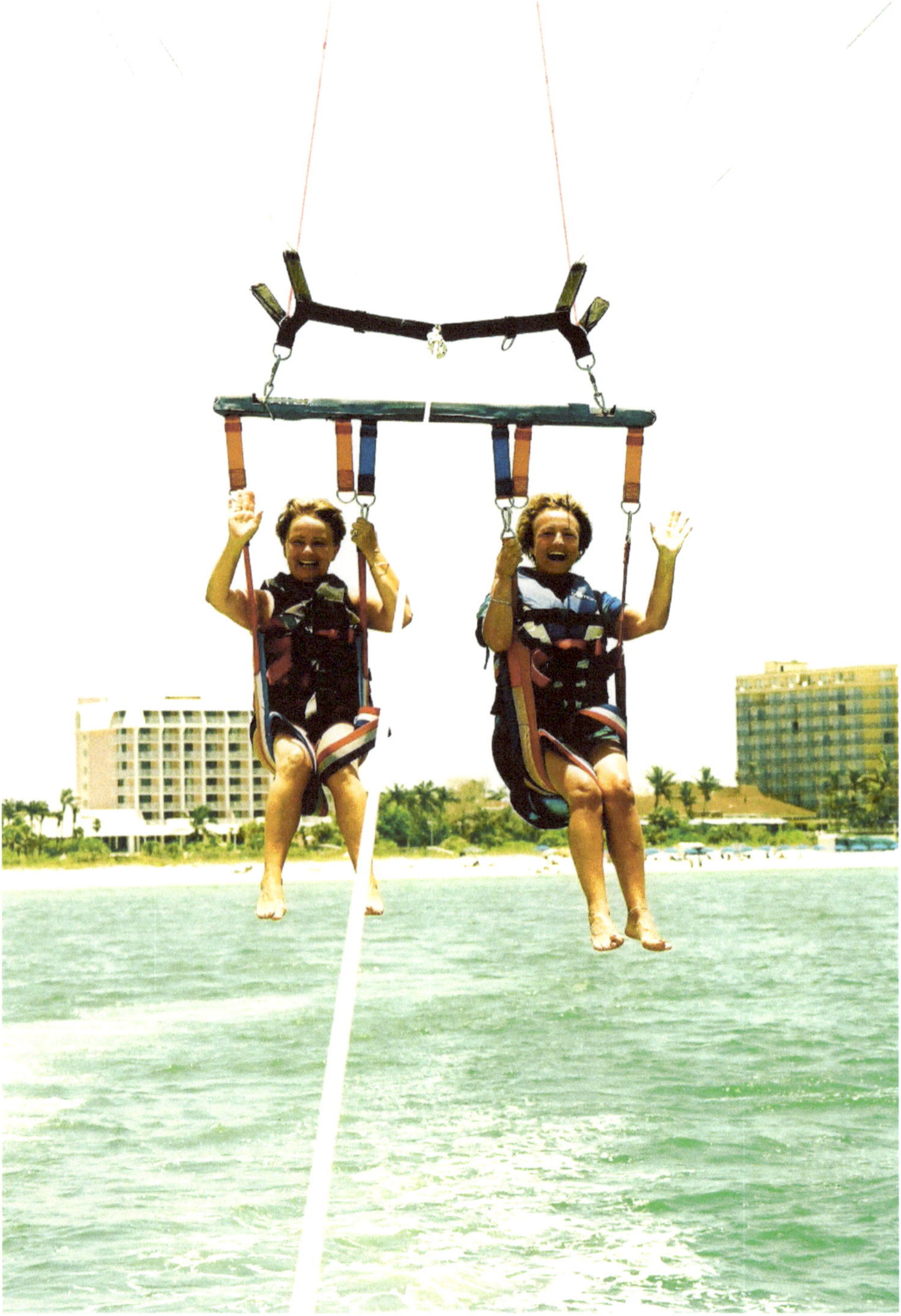

parasailed in **FLORIDA**...

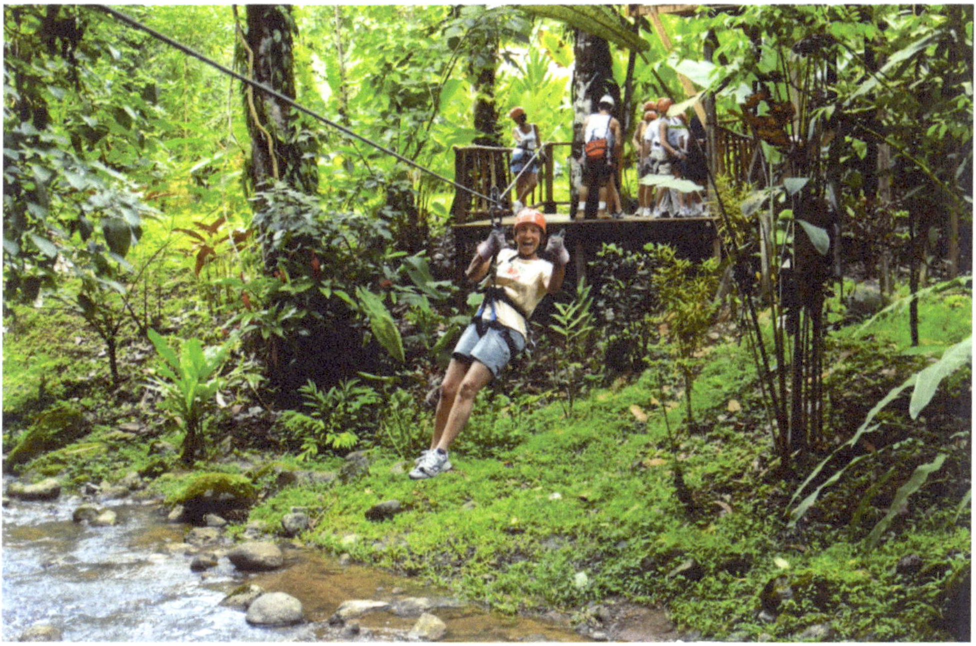

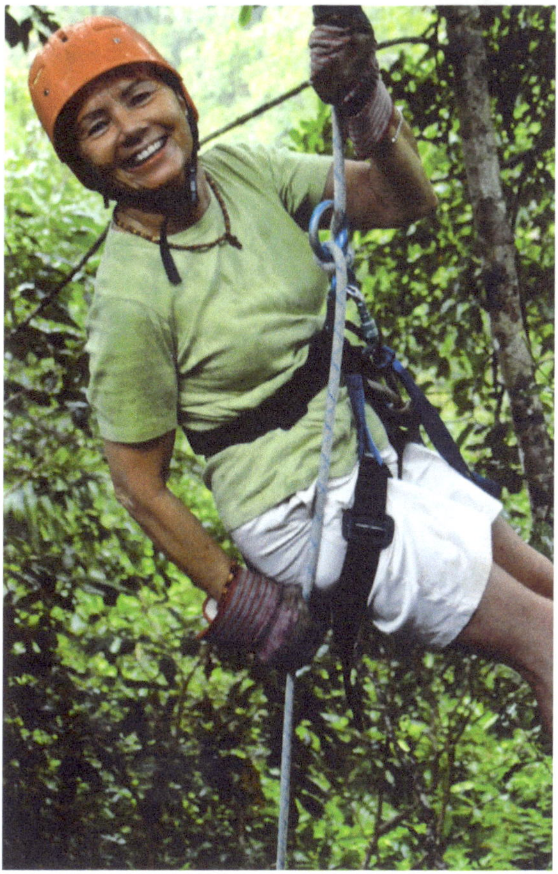

zip-lined...

and repelled in

COSTA RICA...

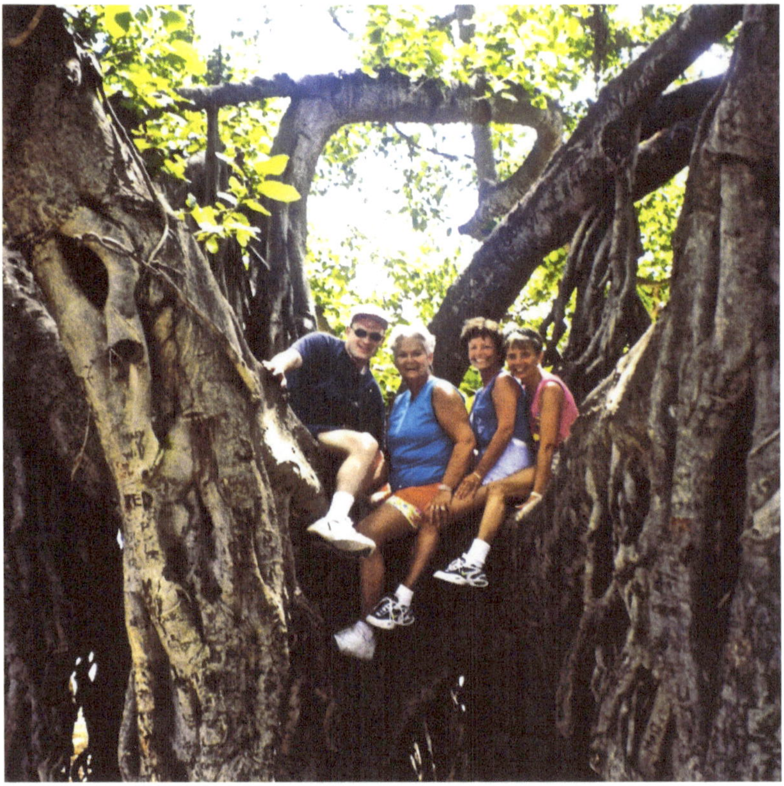

climbed a **BANYAN TREE**...

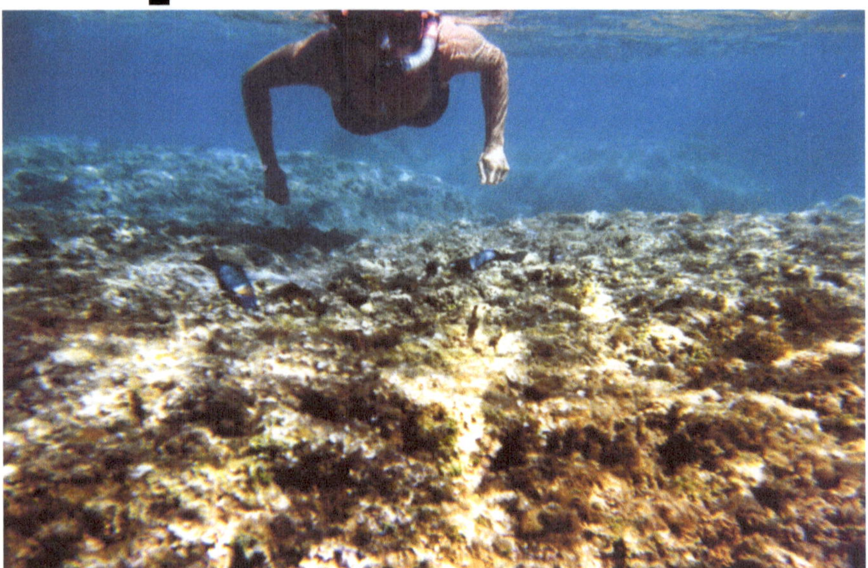

and snorkeled the reefs of **HAWAII**...

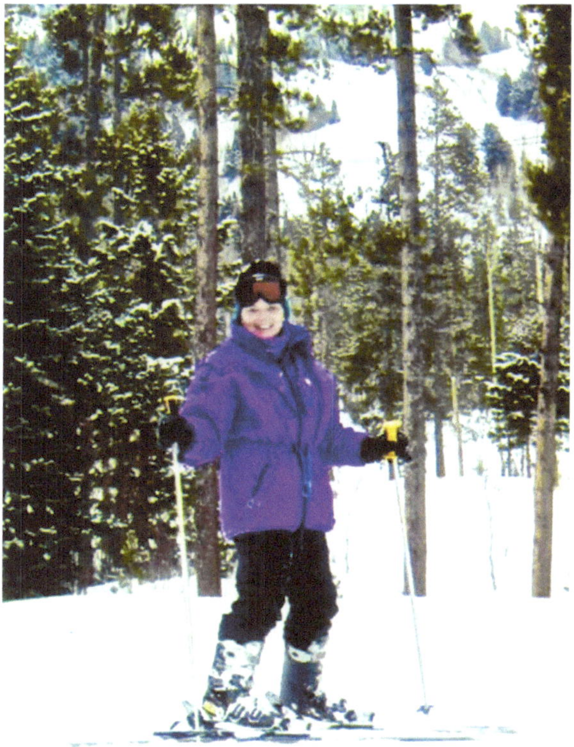

went skiing...

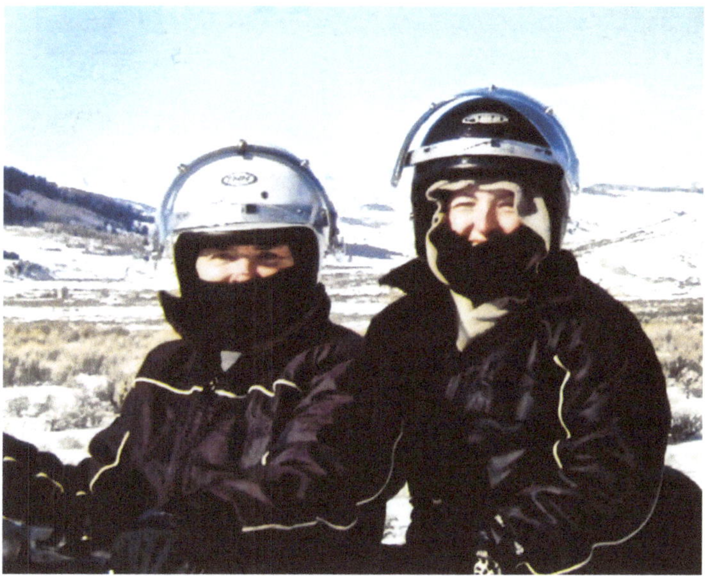

and snowmobiling across the **TETON'S TOWERING PEAKS**...

swam with
dolphins in
MEXICO
and
DOMINICAN REPUBLIC...

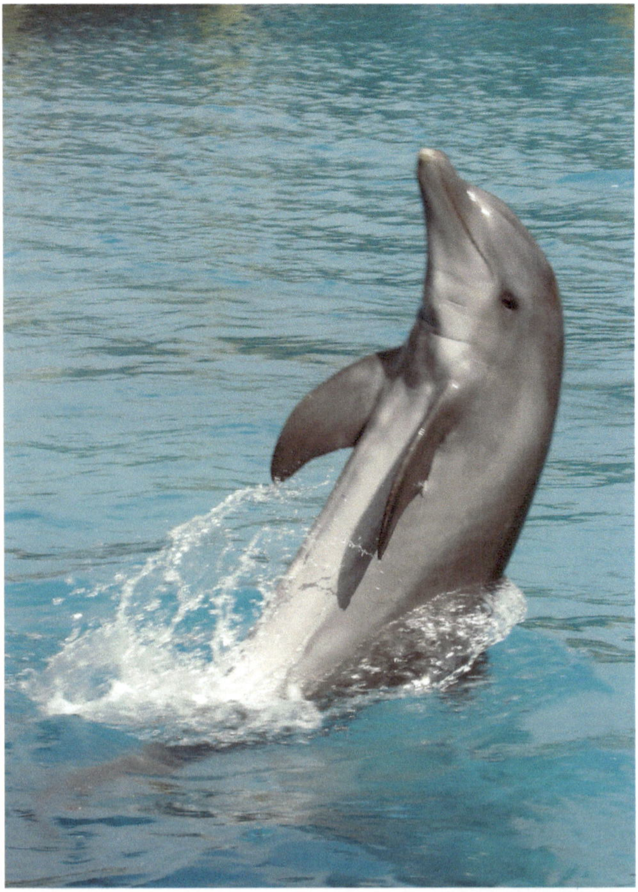

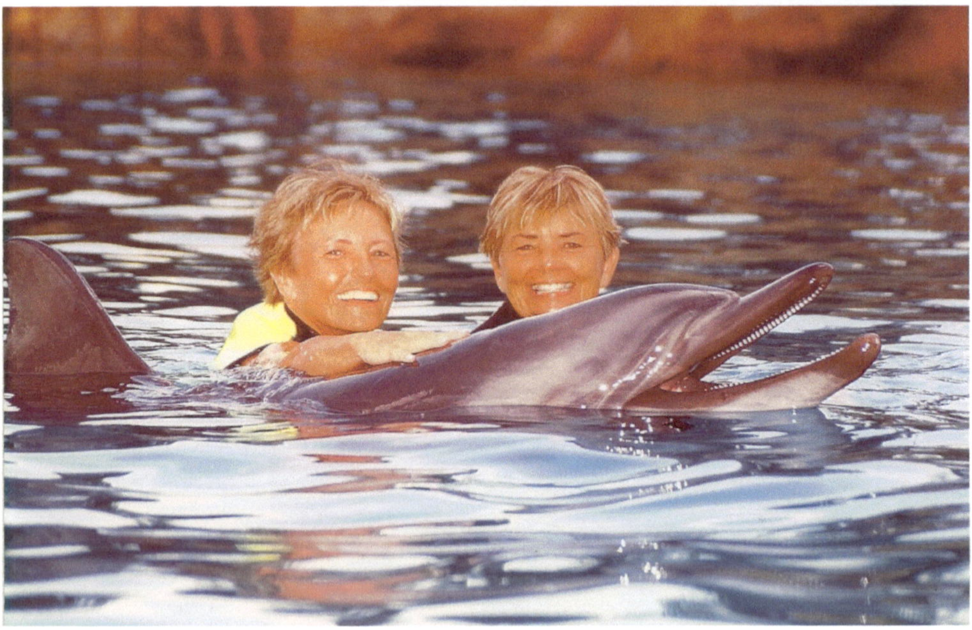

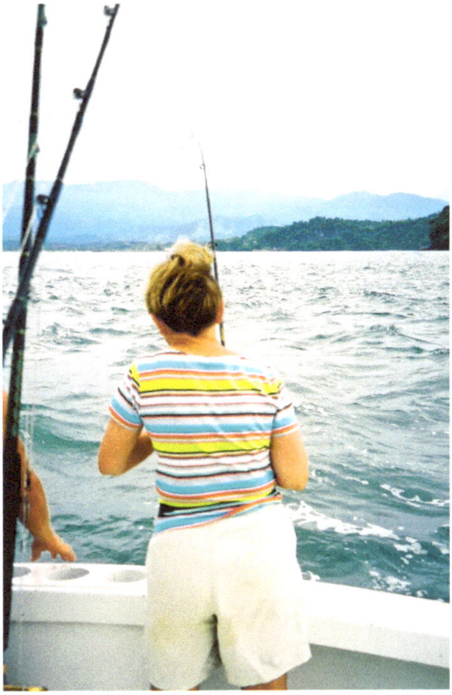

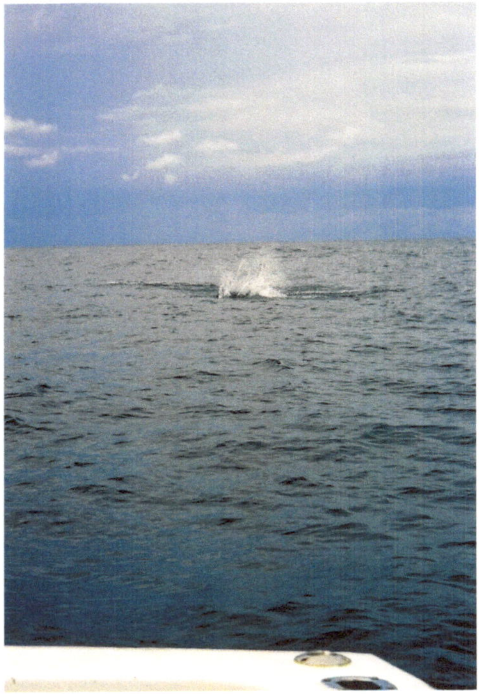

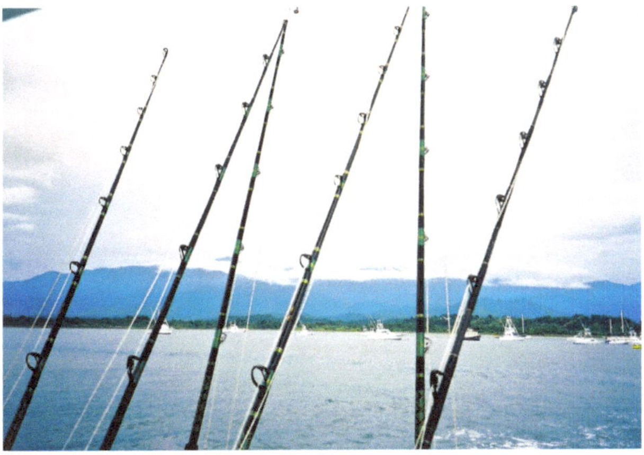

I caught a marlin
while
deep-sea fishing in
COSTA RICA...

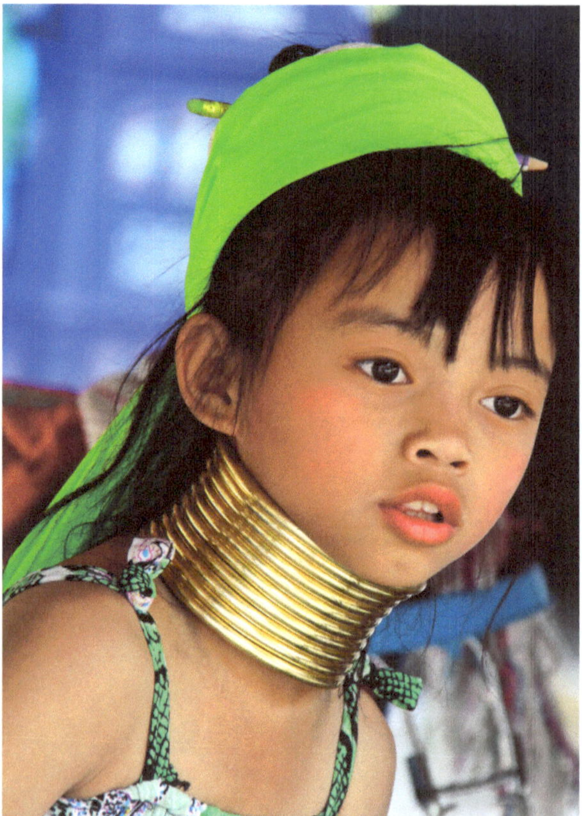

I traveled to the outlying settlements of **THAILAND'S** minority people...

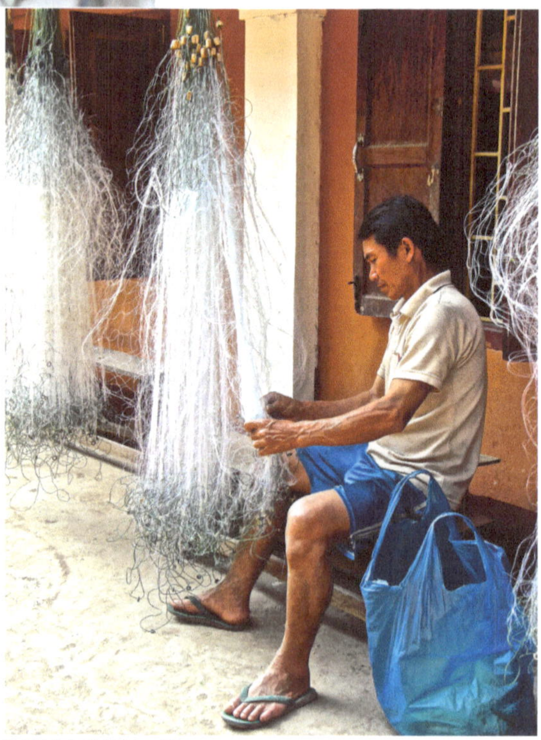

to **LAOS' HILLSIDE** farmers and fishermen...

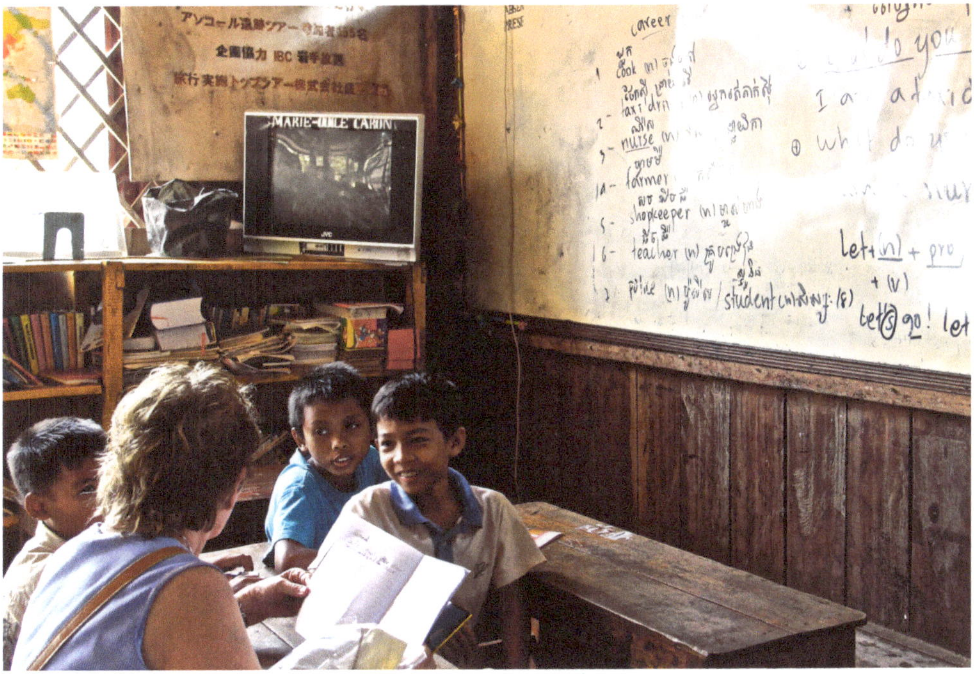

I taught an English class to orphans who were eager to learn in **CAMBODIA**...

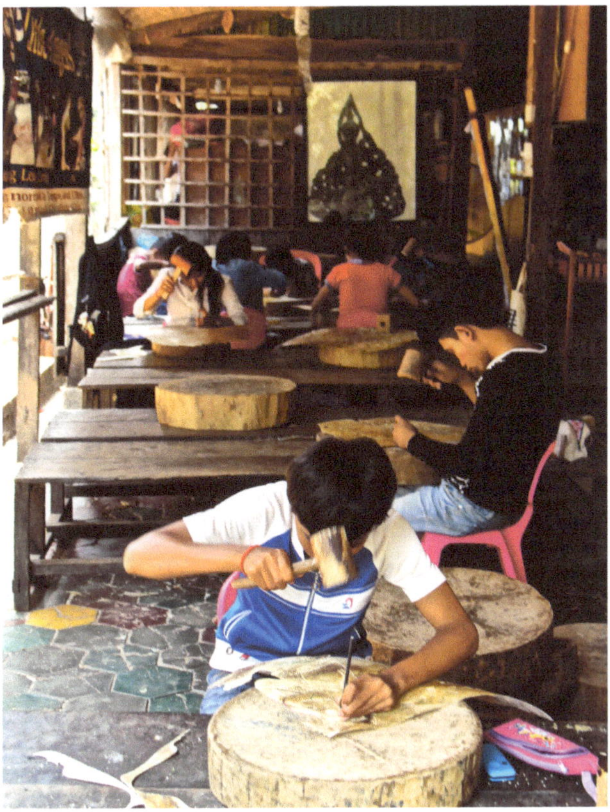

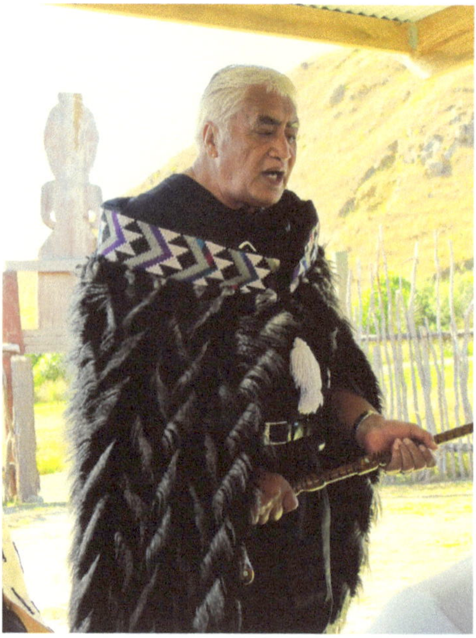

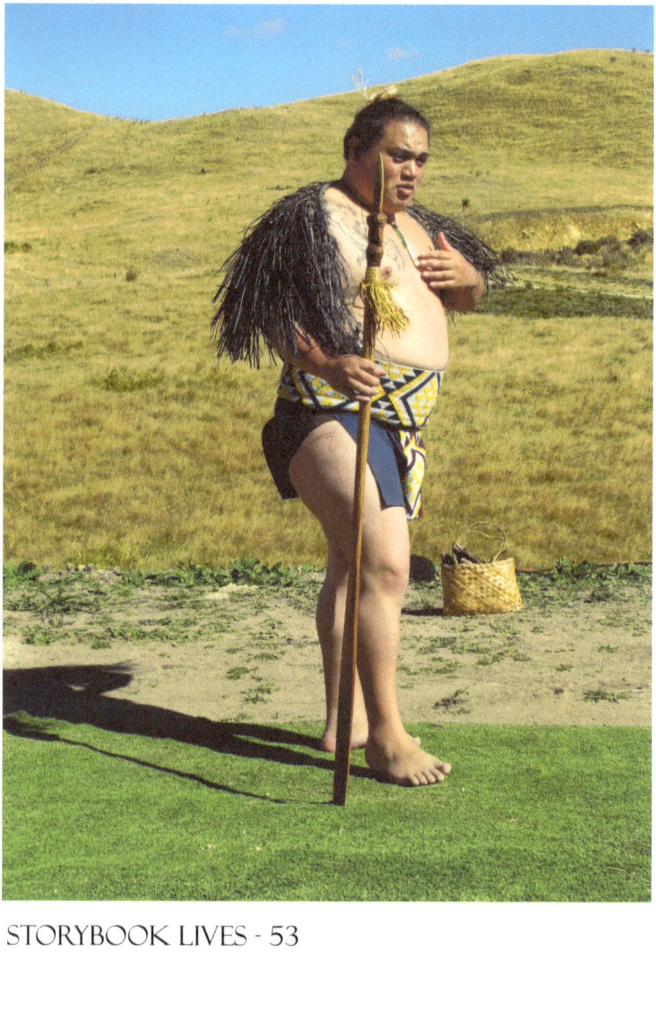

I listened to the lore of

MAORI TRADITIONS...

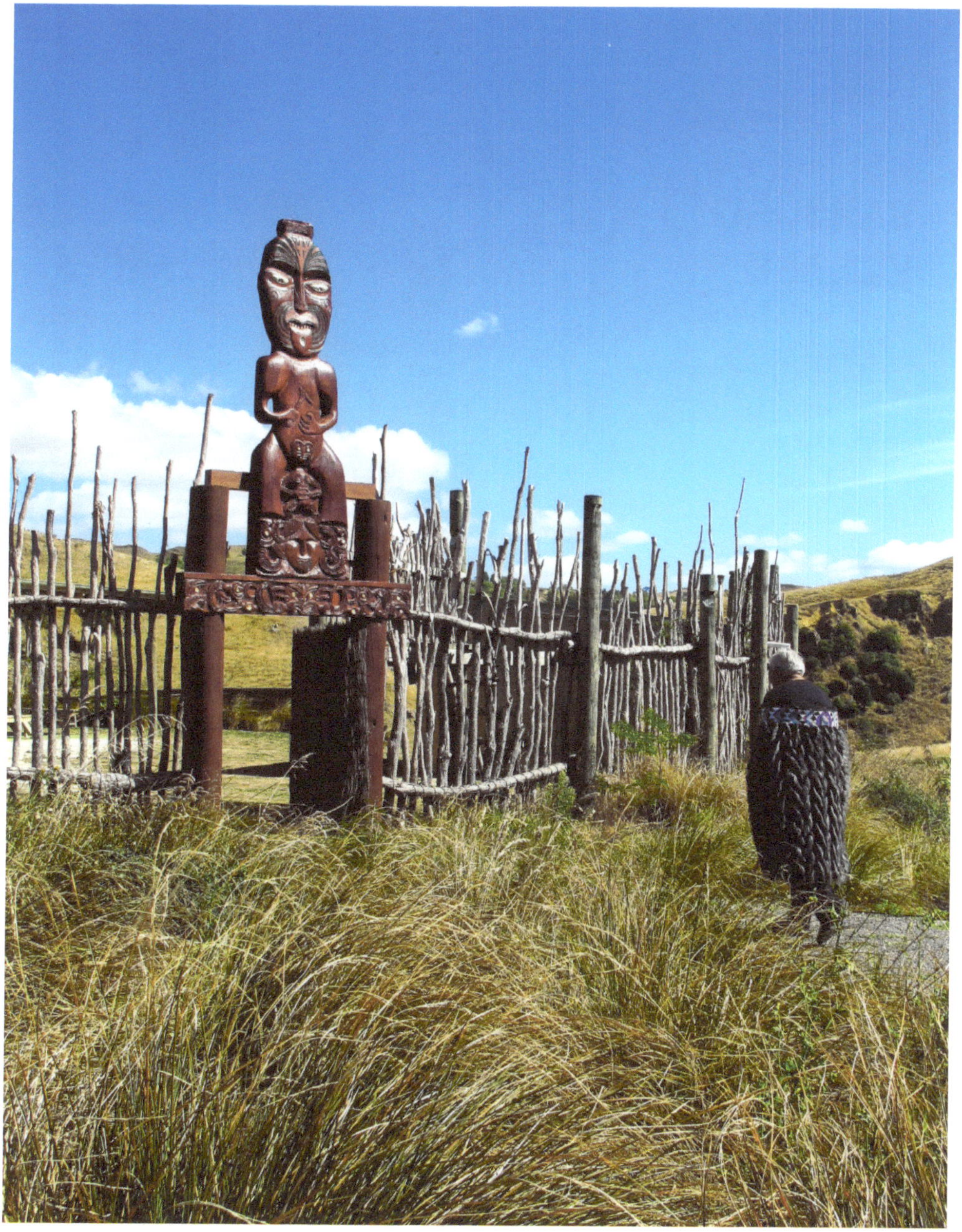

and visited their

POLYNESIAN SETTLEMENT

in New Zealand...

I met the
tribal people
of a
SAMBURU VILLAGE
in the arid lands
of Kenya...

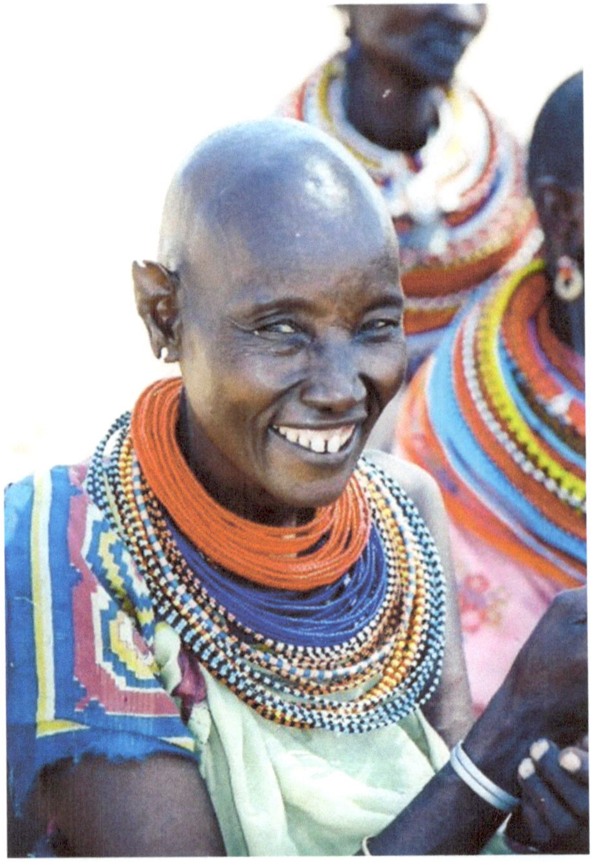

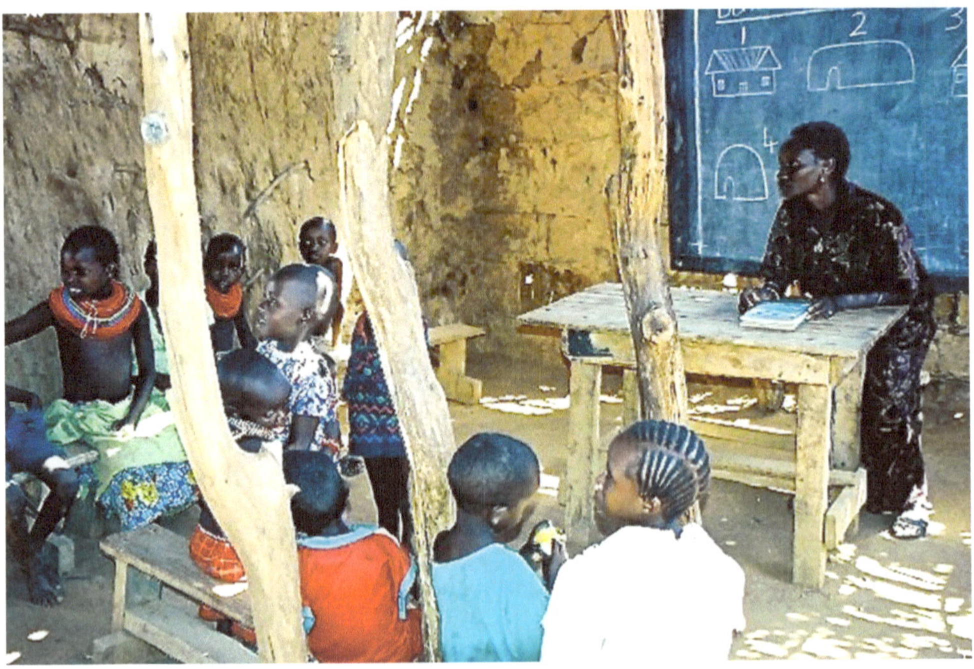

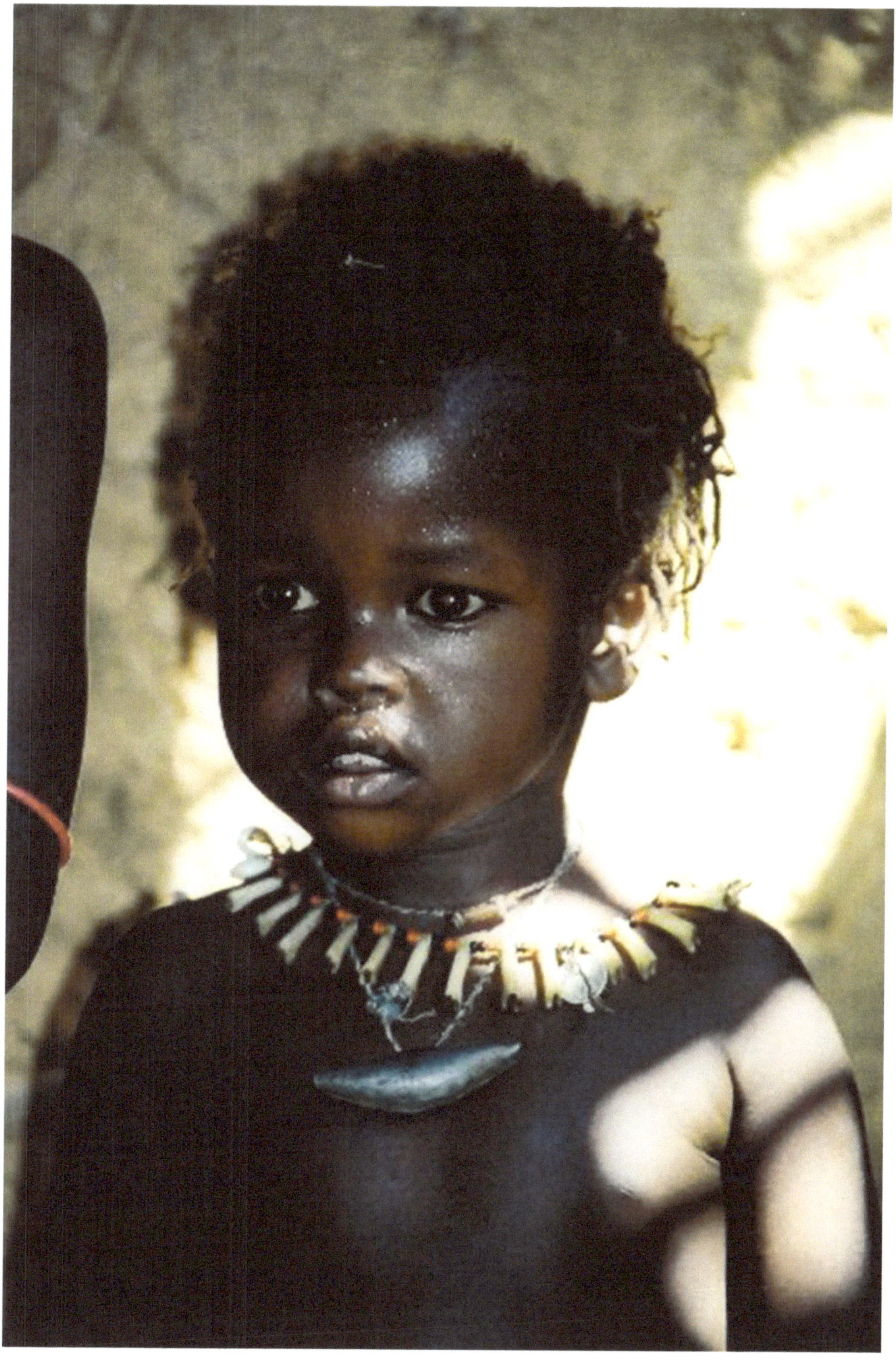

and a
MASSAI
VILLAGE
in the Serengeti...

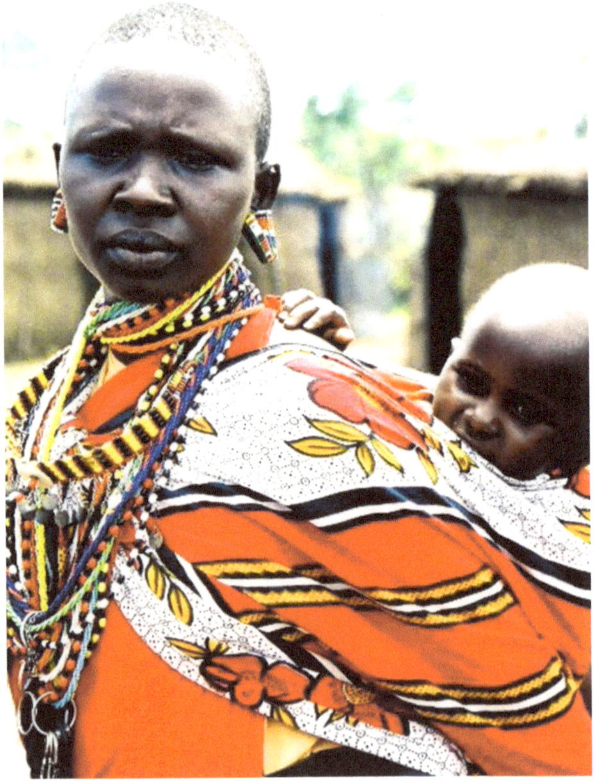

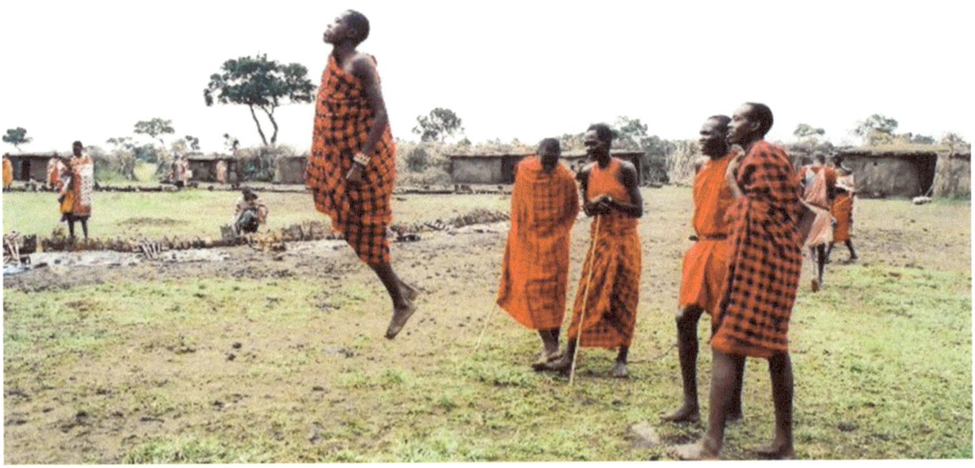

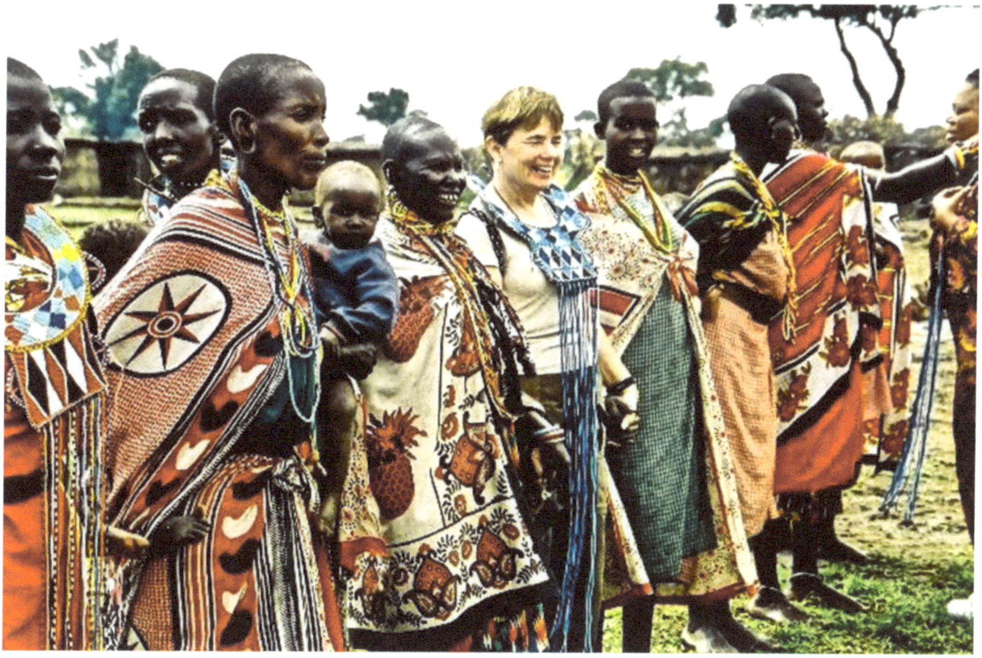

and even had a **MASSAI MATRIARCH**
offer to build us a hut...

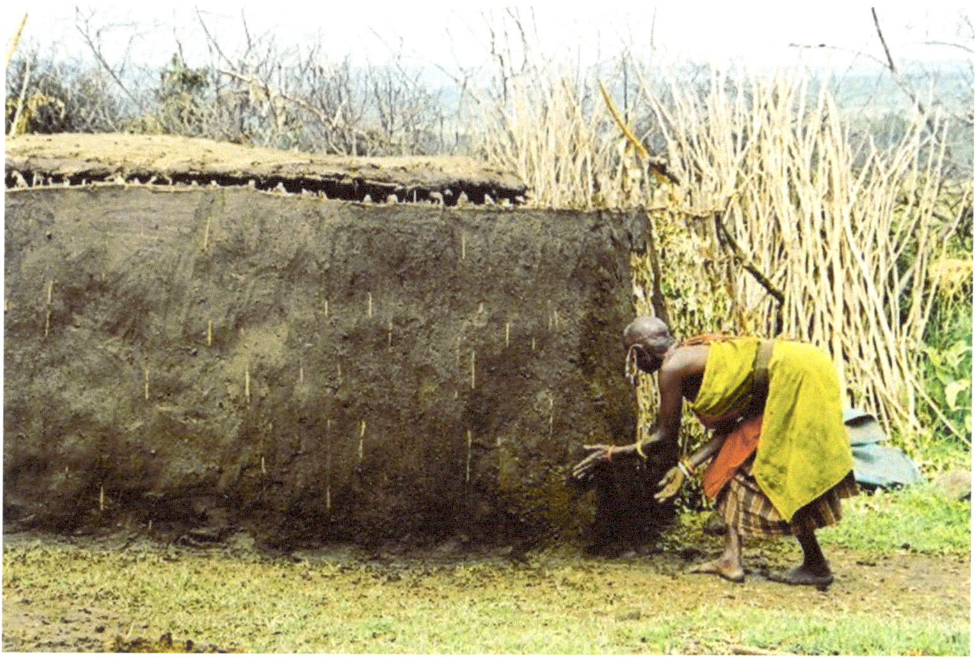

I listened to war stories by fireside in the **FALKLANDS**...

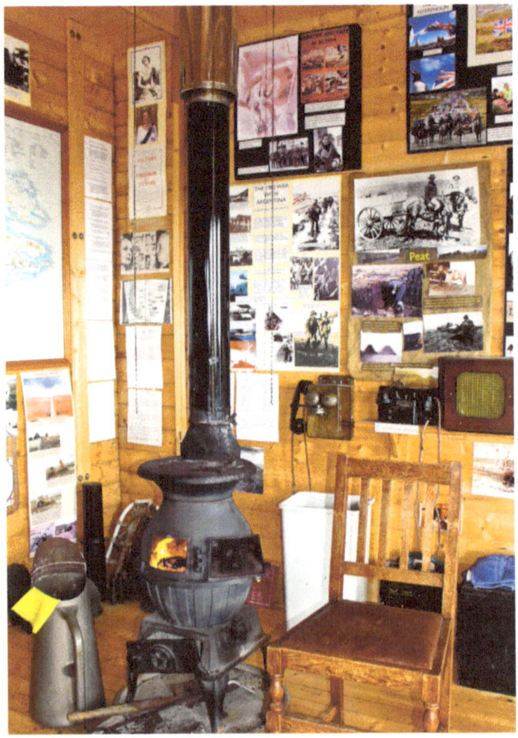

I saw evidence of **SERBIA'S** rebuilding...

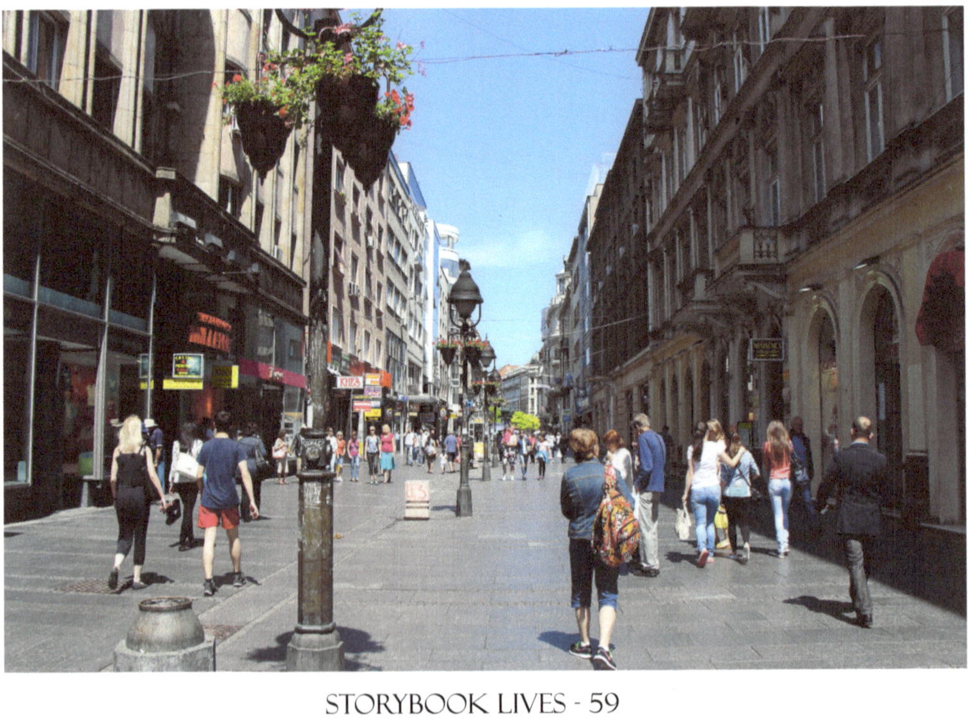

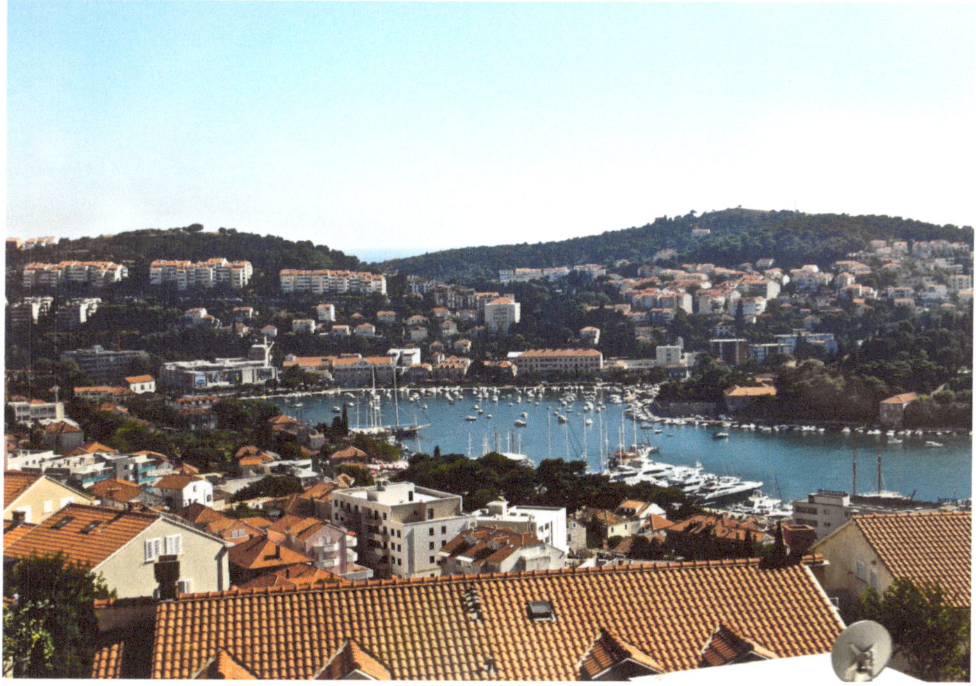

and CROATIA'S DIVISIONS...

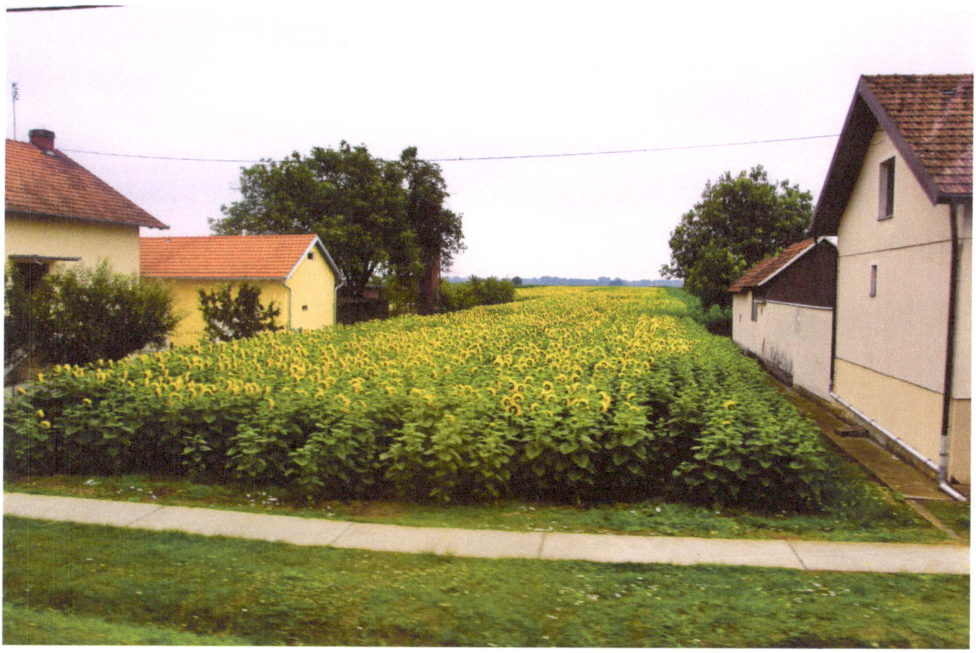

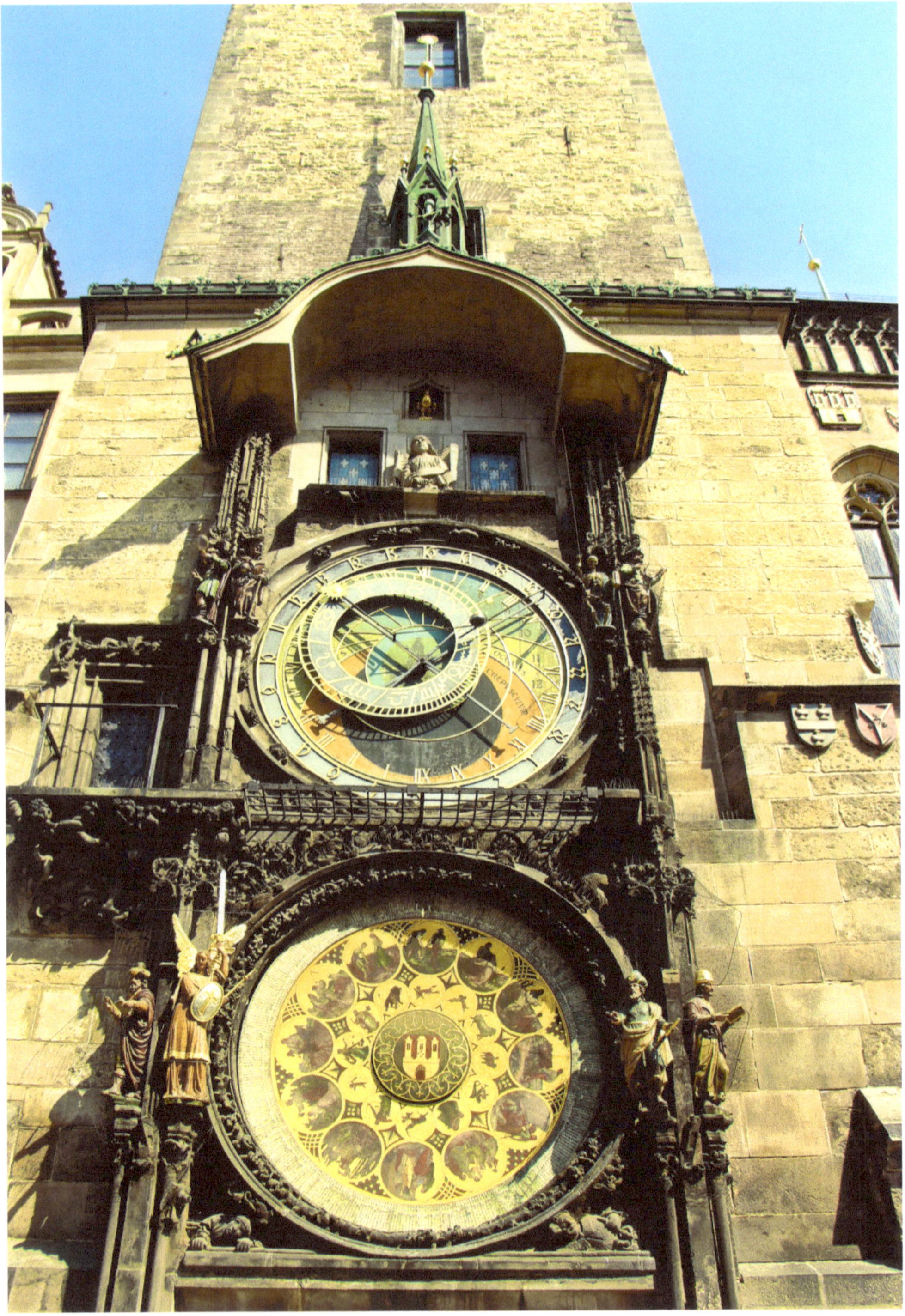

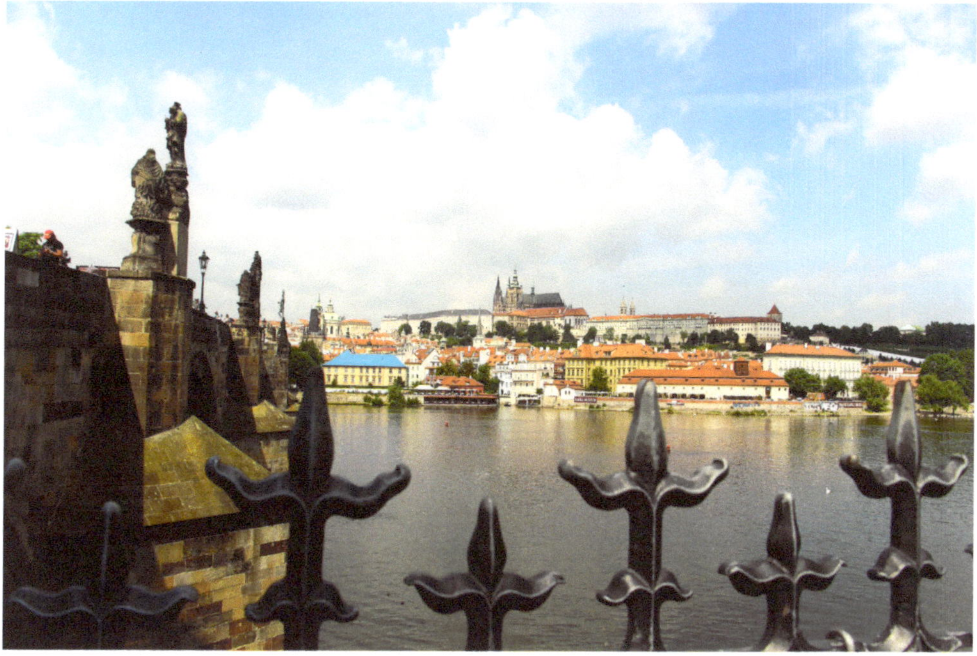

and the memorials in **PRAGUE**...

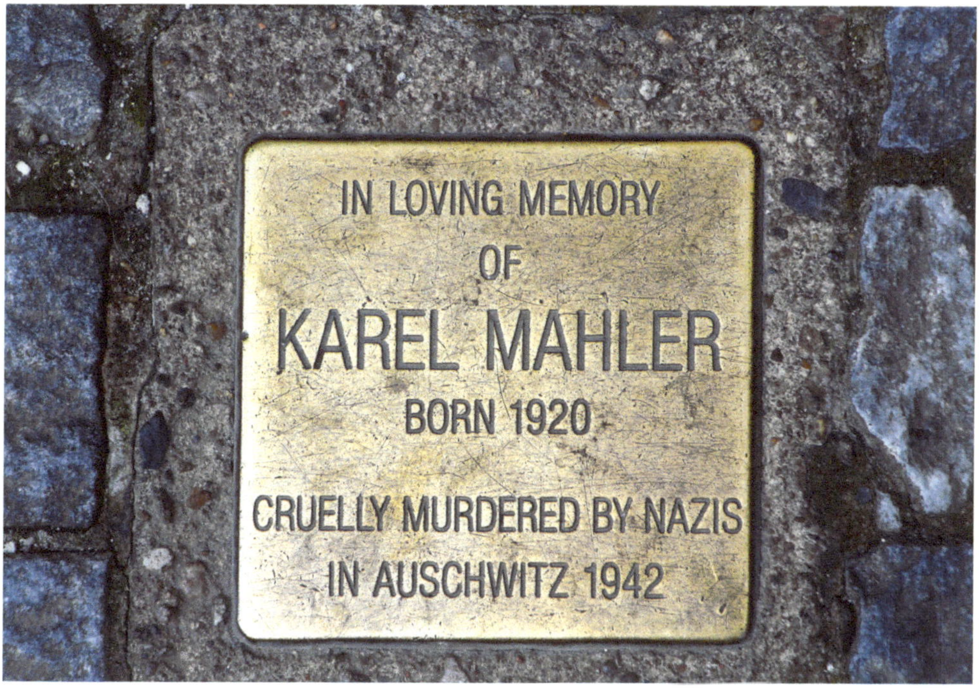

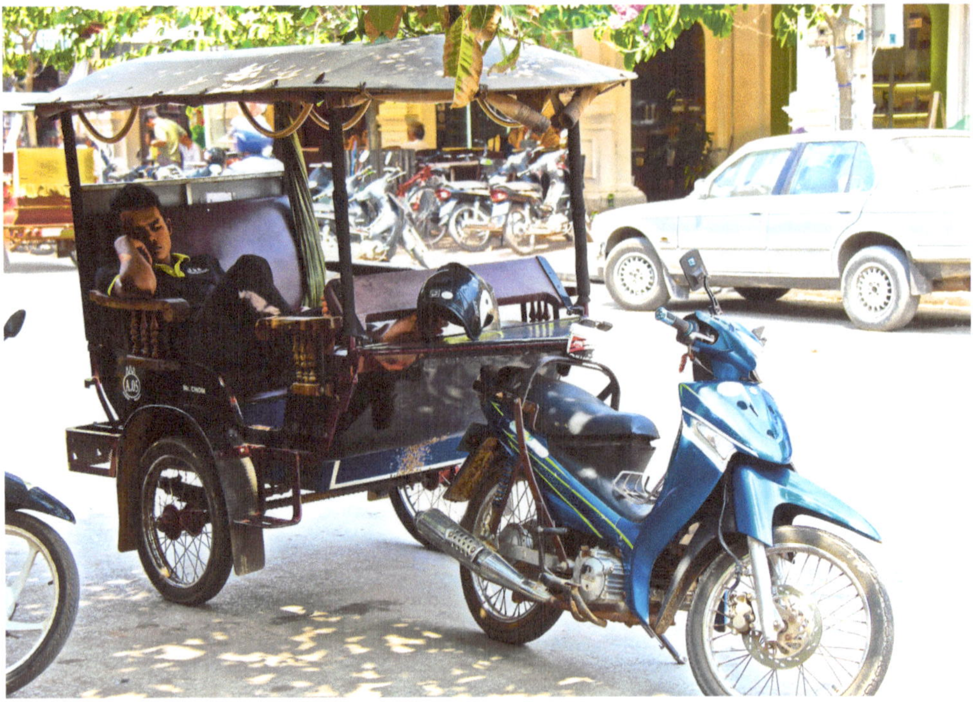

took a tuk-tuk to

CAMBODIA'S TEMPLES...

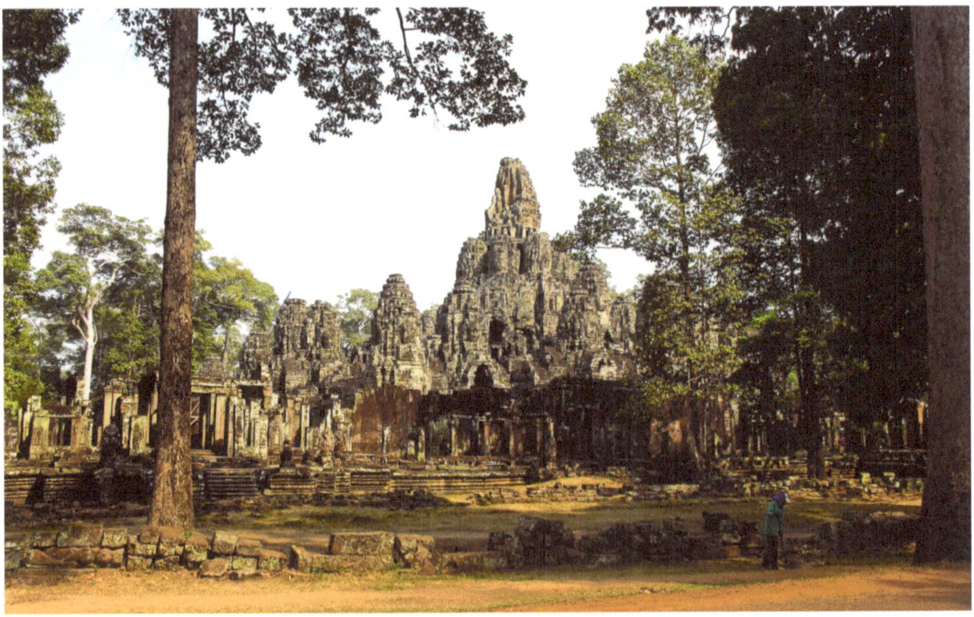

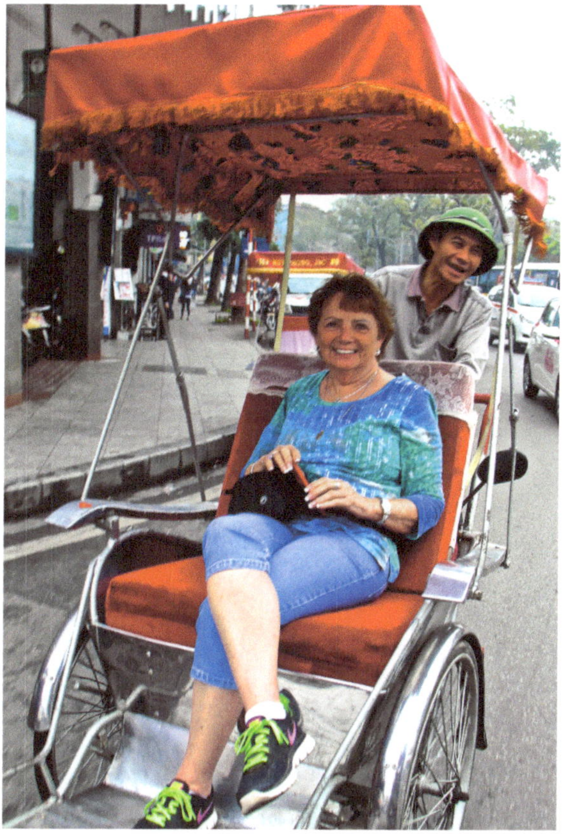

rode a rickshaw
through the
afternoon
marketplace of
HANOI...

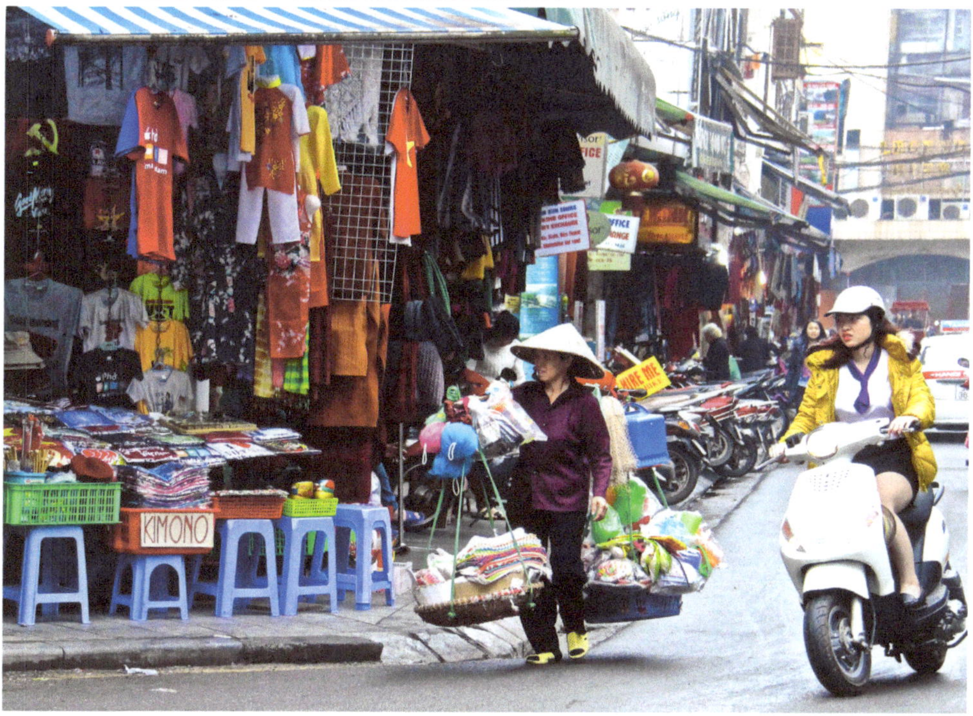

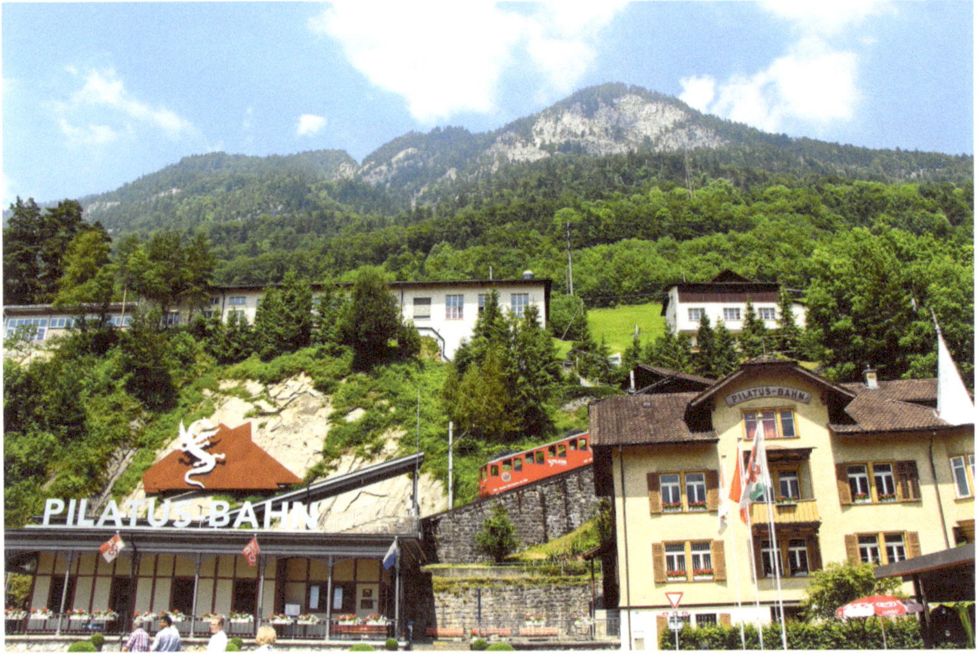

I took the world's steepest cogwheel railway to the peak of **PILATUS IN LUCERNE**...

and the equally steep cabled tram down...

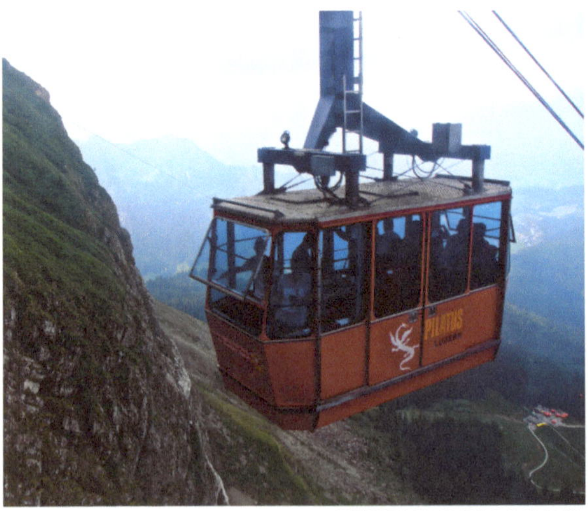

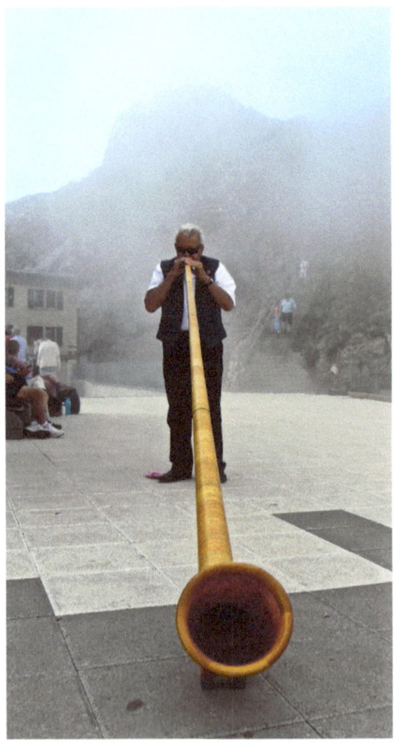

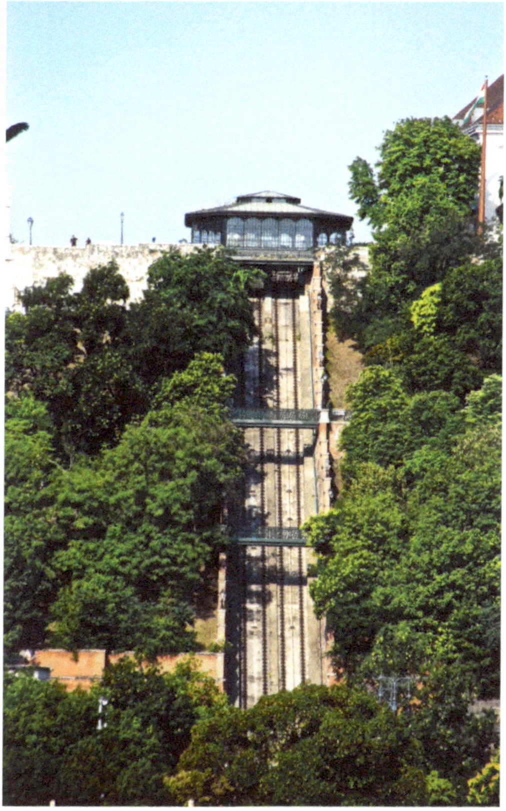

I rode a funicular from

BUDAPEST'S

mountaintop

fairytale-like castle...

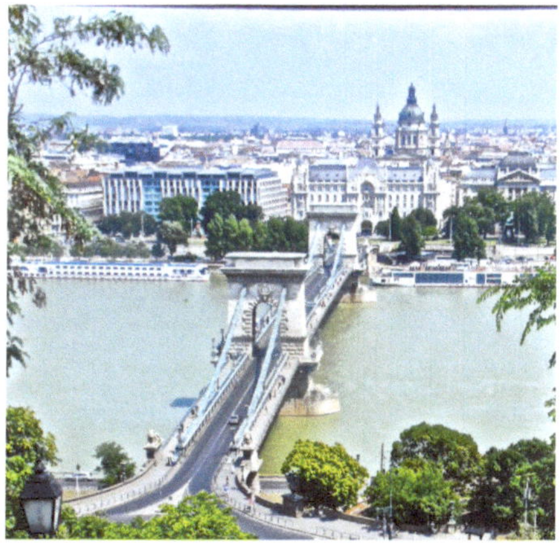

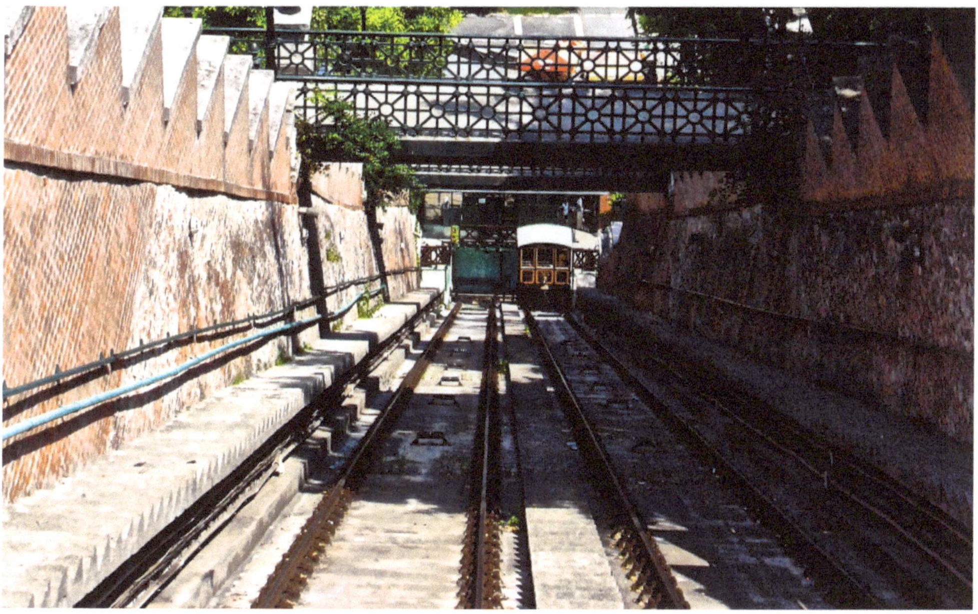

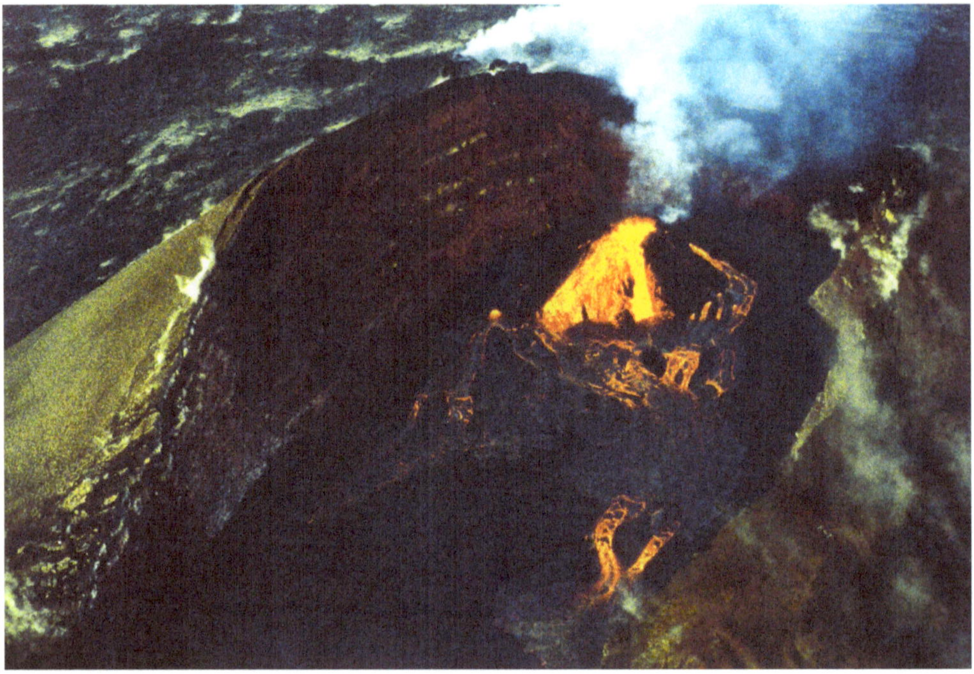

flew over

HAWAII'S

active volcano...

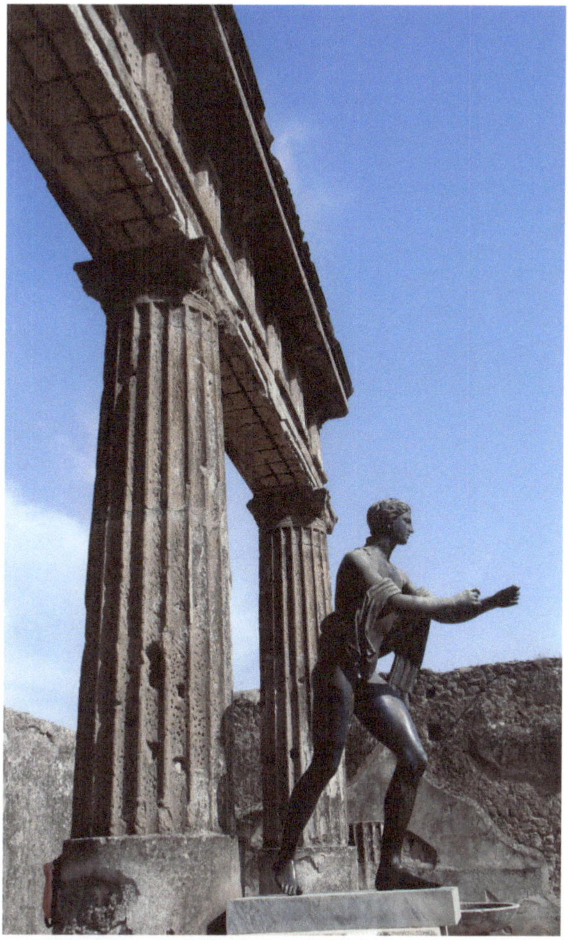

I saw the result of the volcanic devastation of Pompeii's **MT. VESUVIUS**...

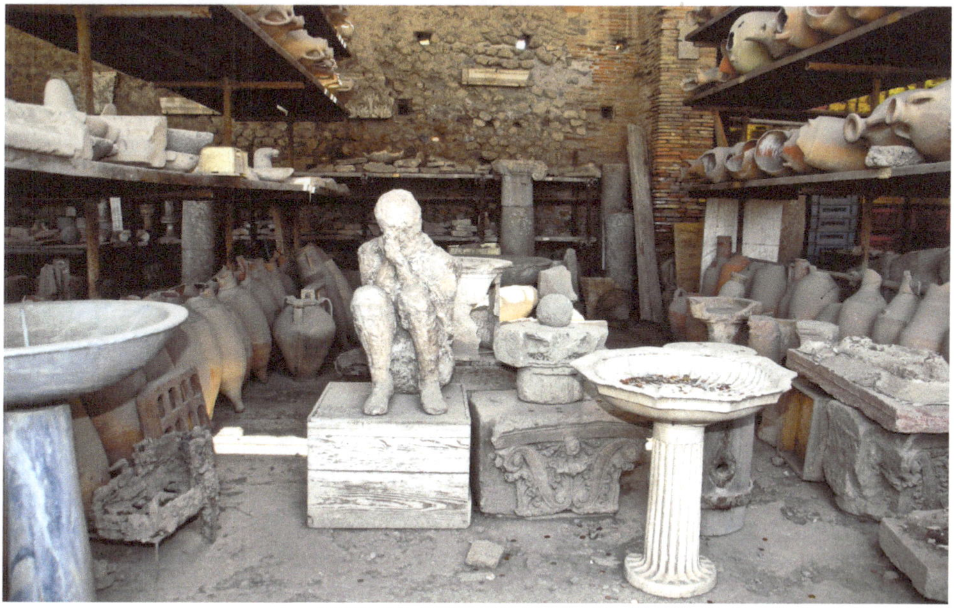

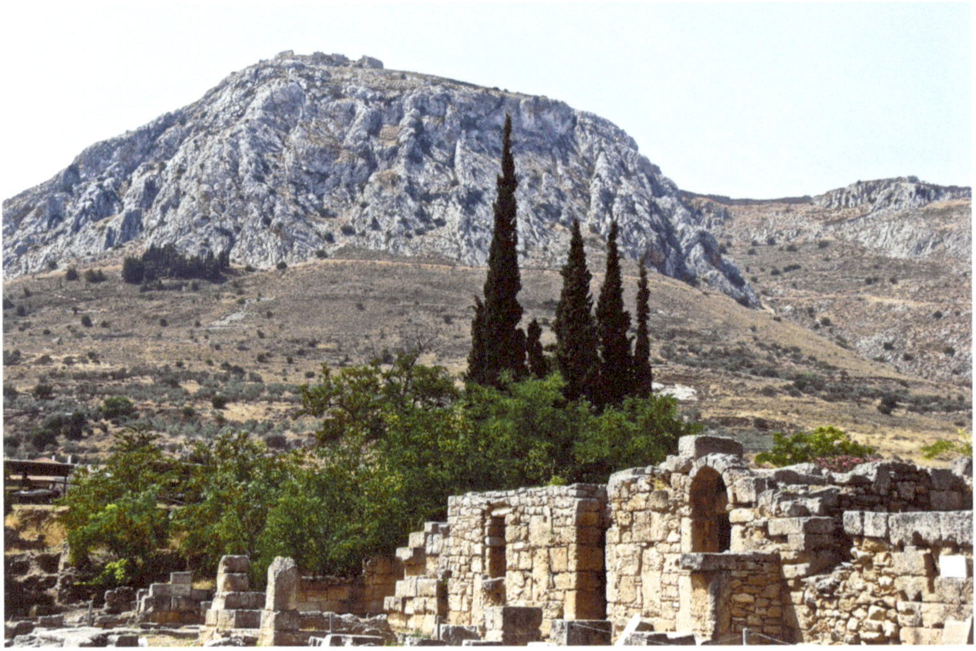

I walked the dusty roads of the **APOSTLE PAUL** through the ancient city of **CORINTH**...

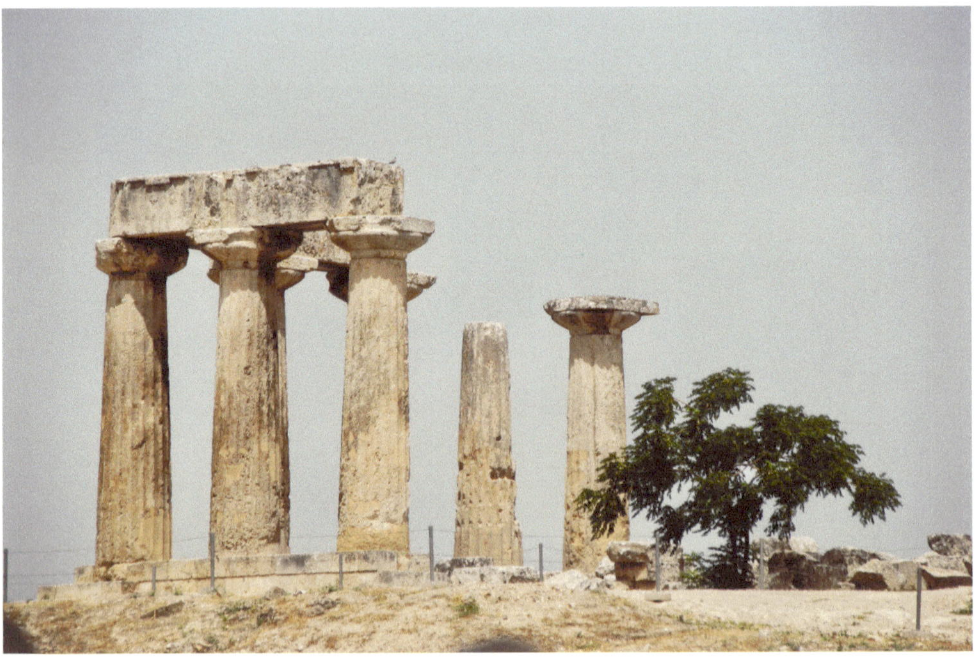

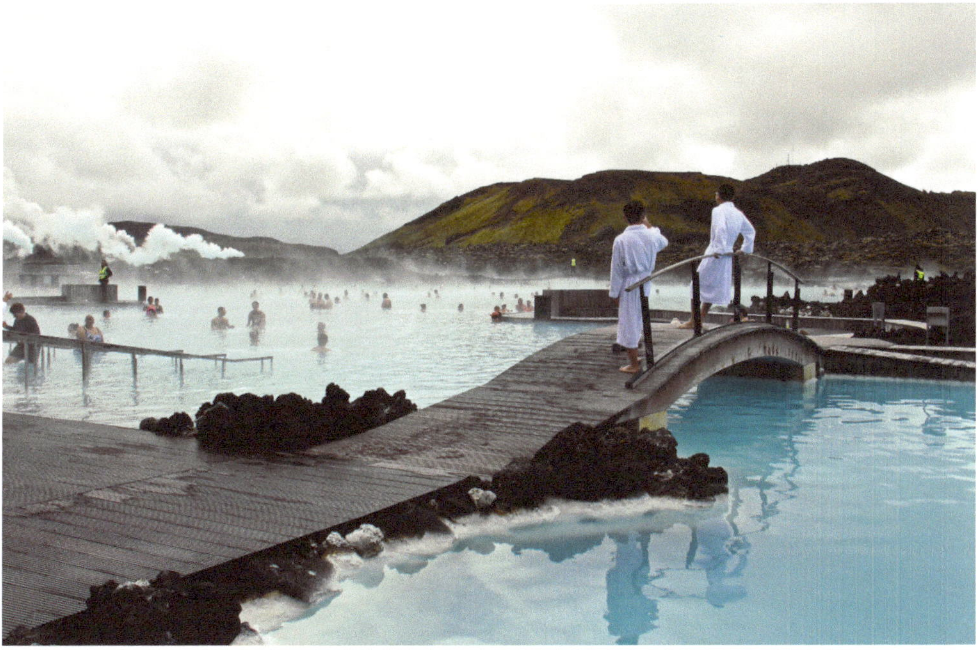

I waded in **ICELAND'S BLUE LAGOON**...

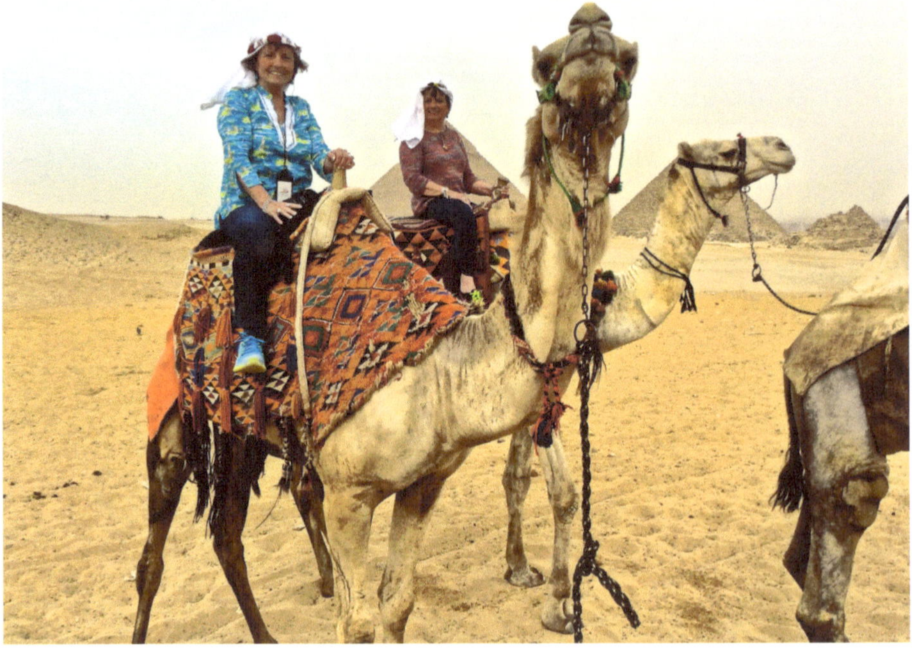

rode camels in **EGYPT'S SAHARA DESERT**
at the site of **THE GREAT PYRAMID**...

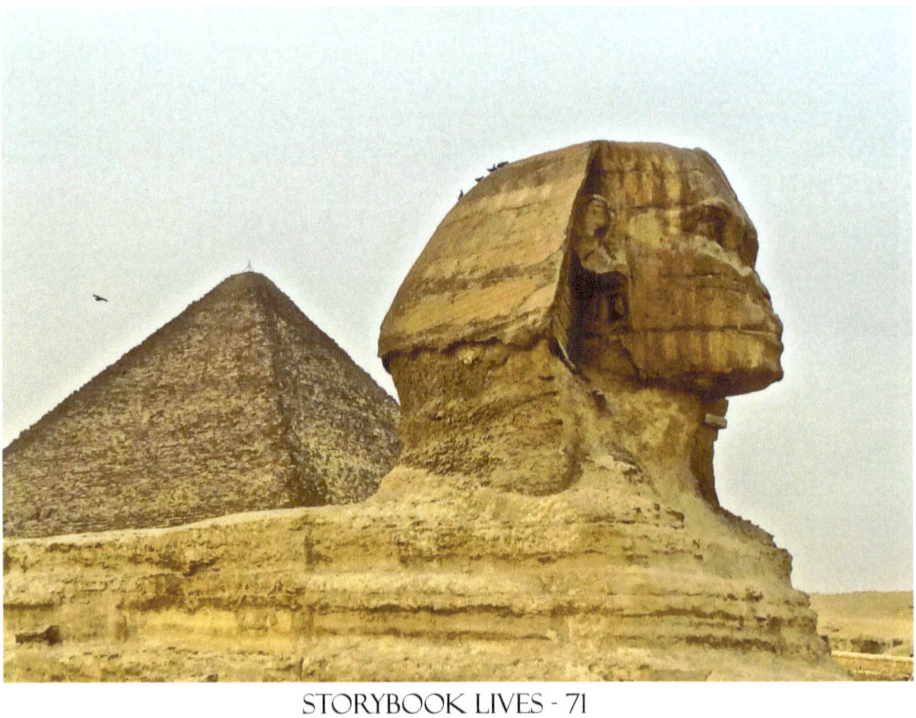

wound our way through Paris streets to the historical **NOTRE DAME CATHEDRAL**...

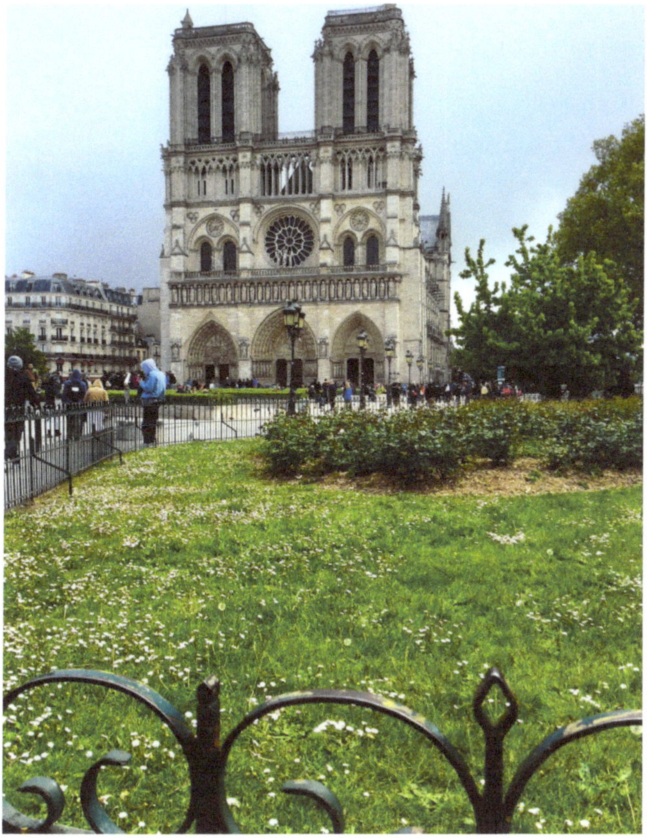

to the famous **LOUVRE MUSEUM**...

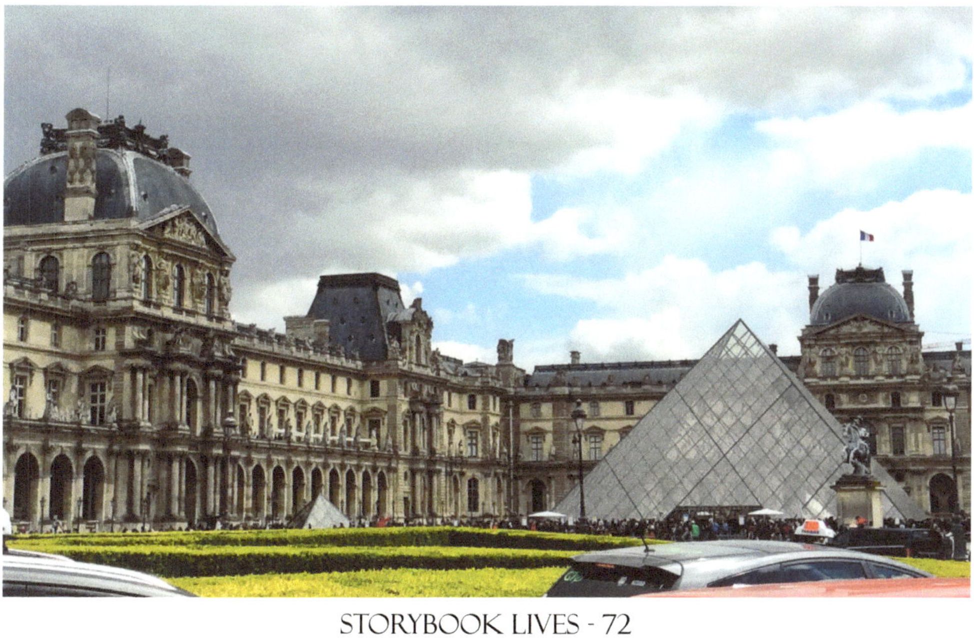

and to
the stunning

EIFFEL TOWER...

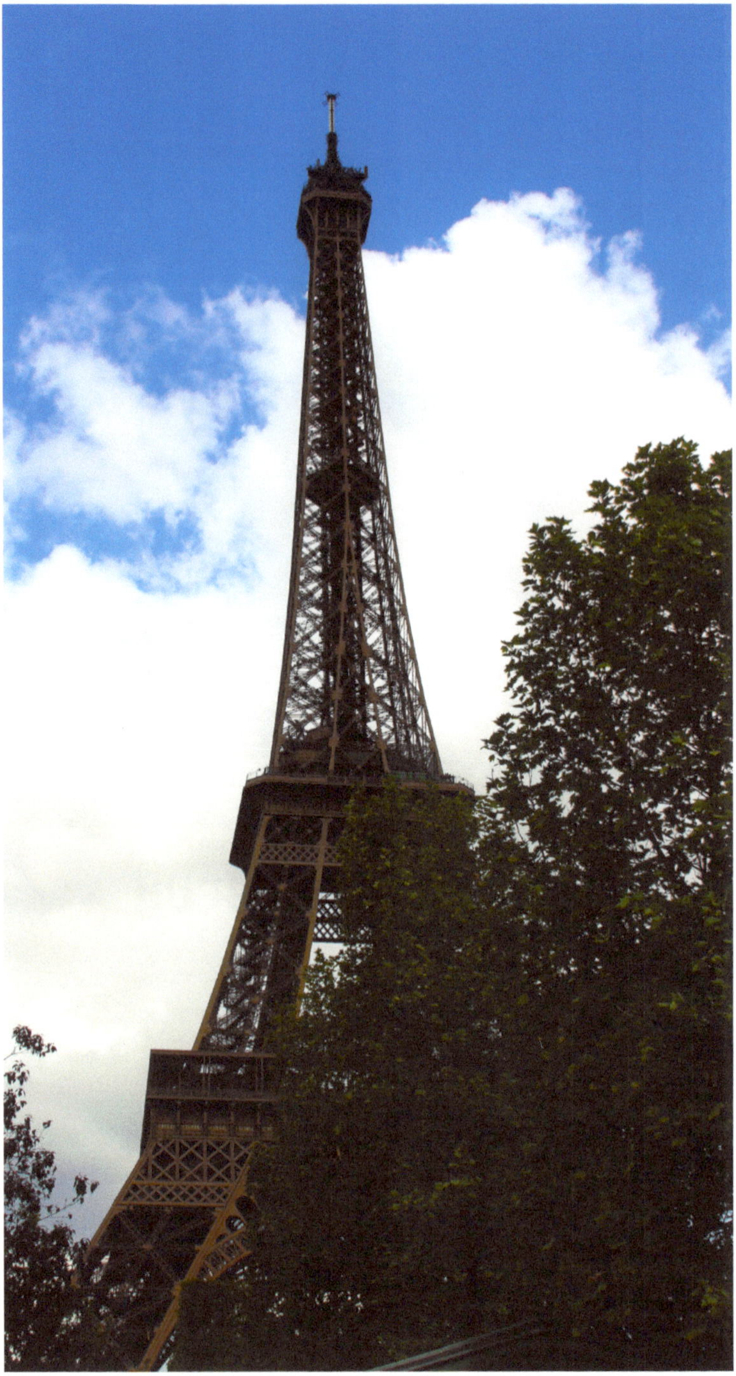

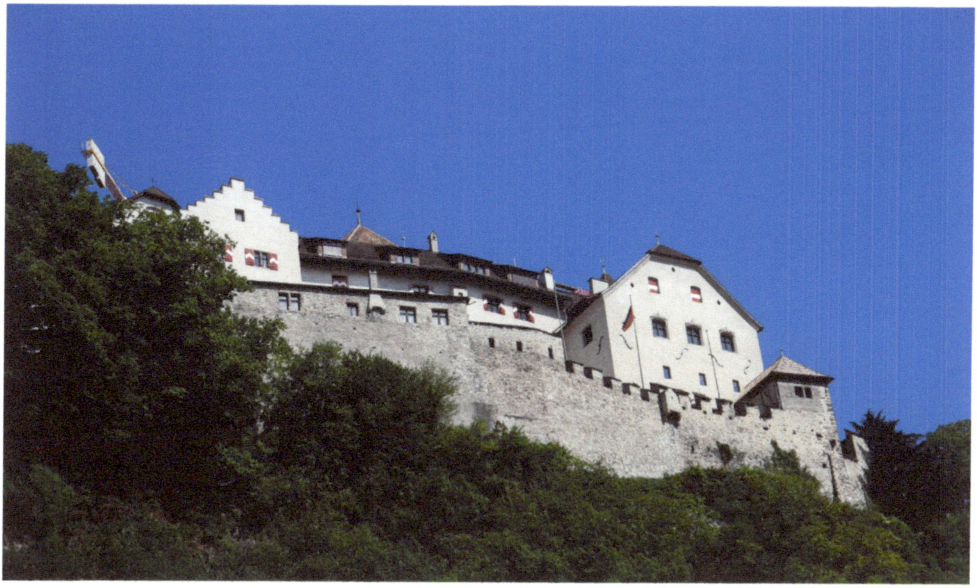

I visited **LICHTENSTEIN**, considered to be the smallest country in the world (excluding Vatican City)...

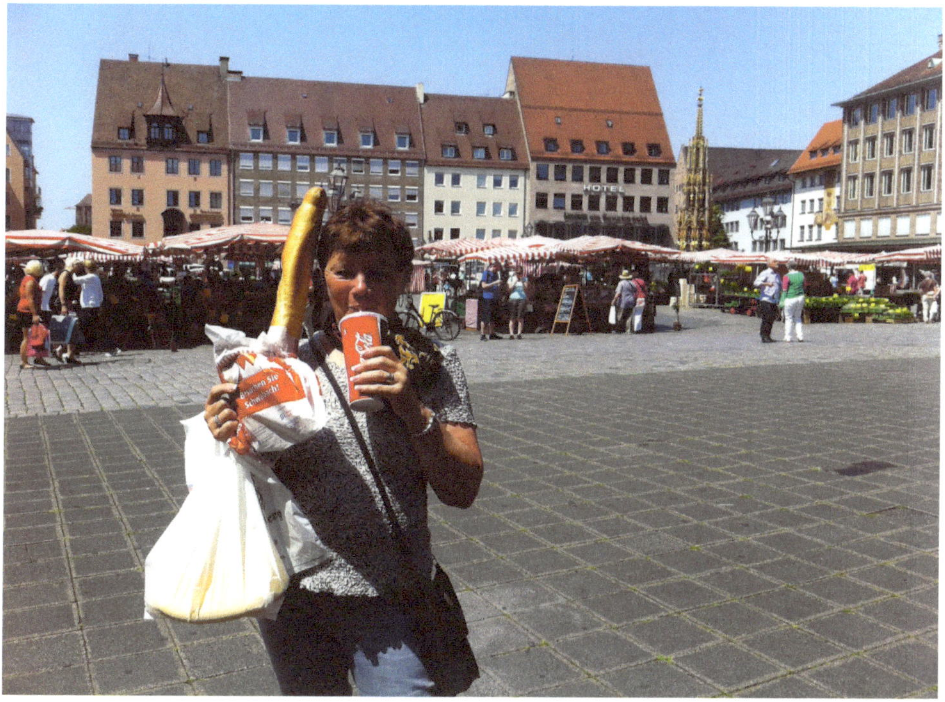

and shopped at **GERMANY'S CHRISTMAS MARKET**...

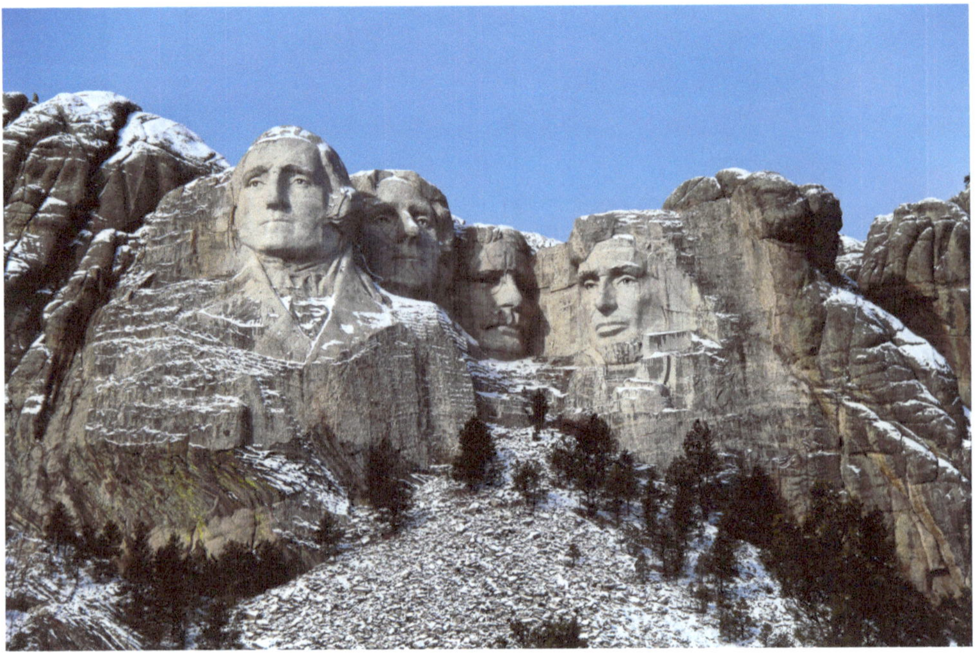

observed the beauty and history of America at the monuments,

from **SOUTH DAKOTA**...

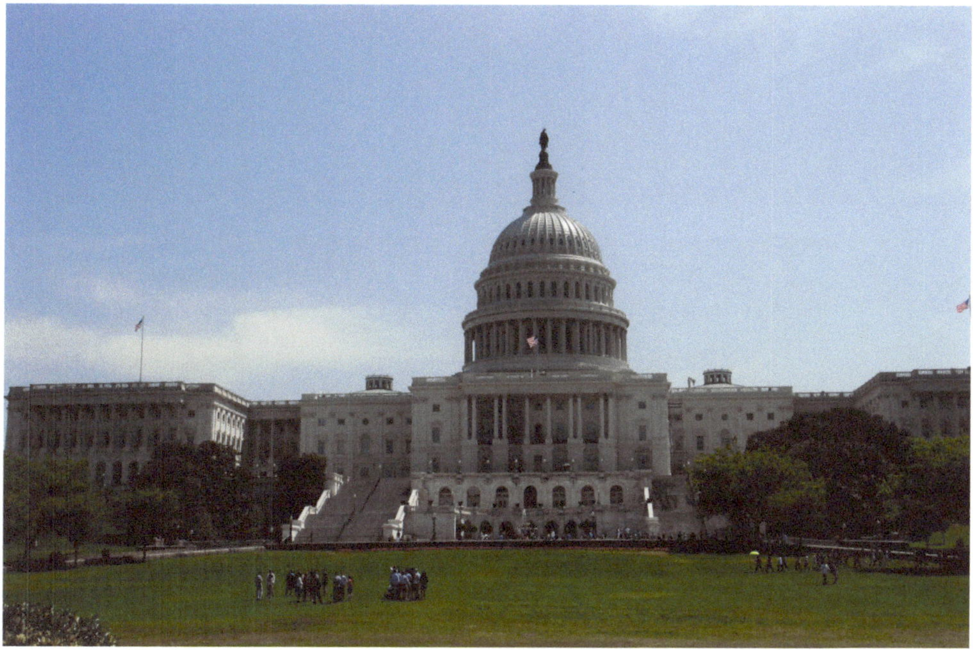

to **WASHINGTON, D.C....**

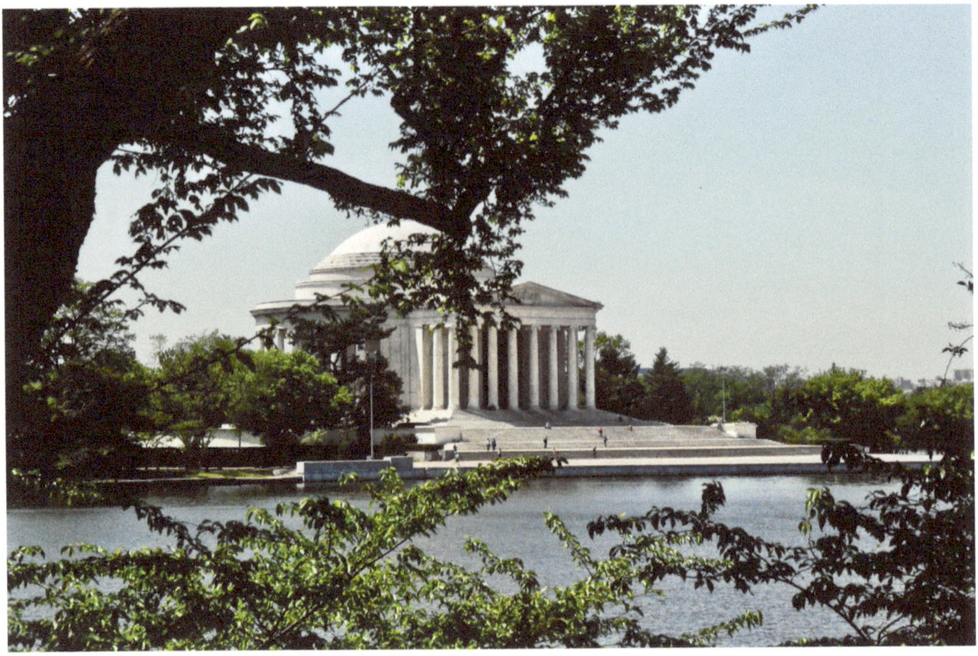

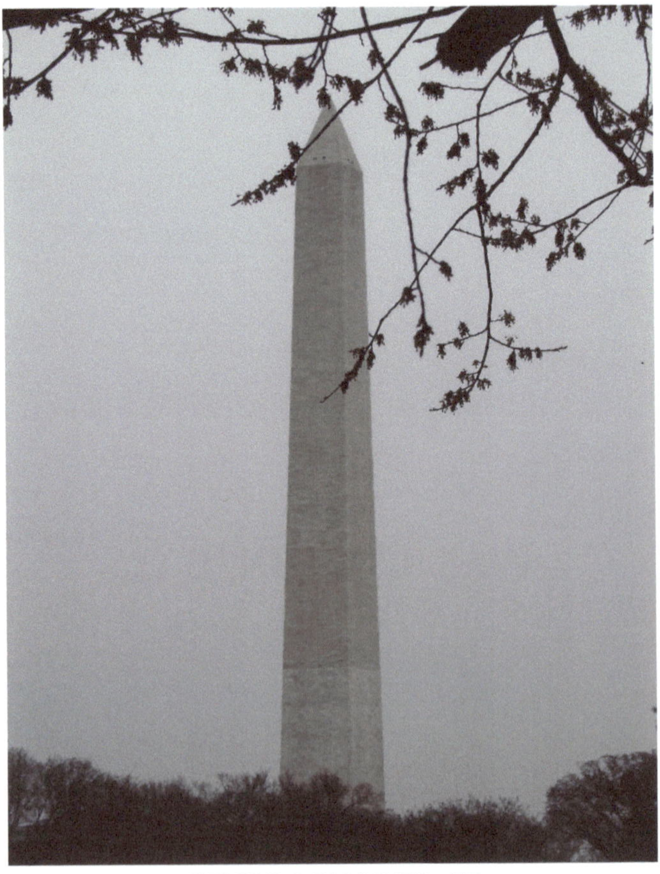

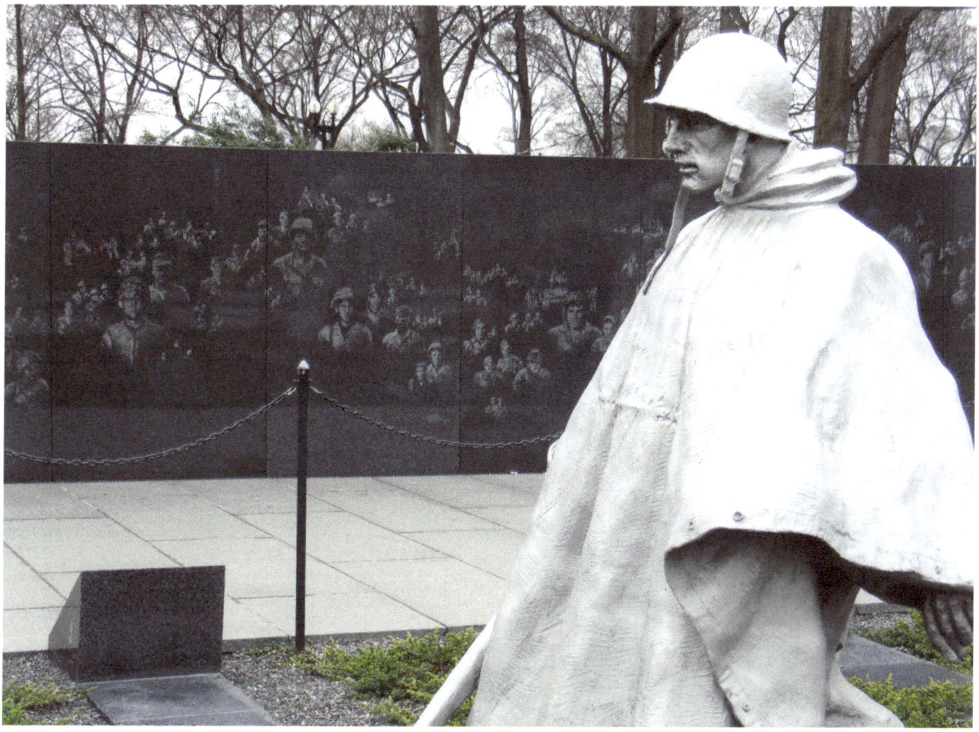

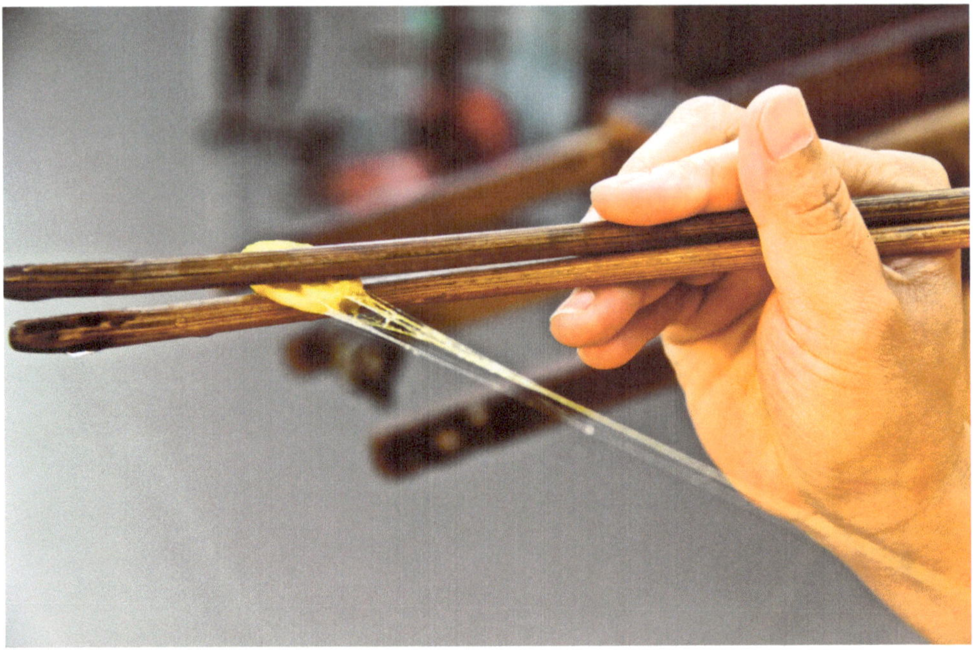

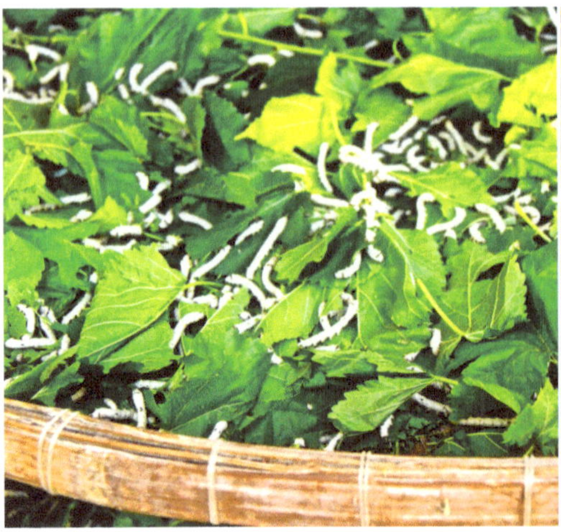

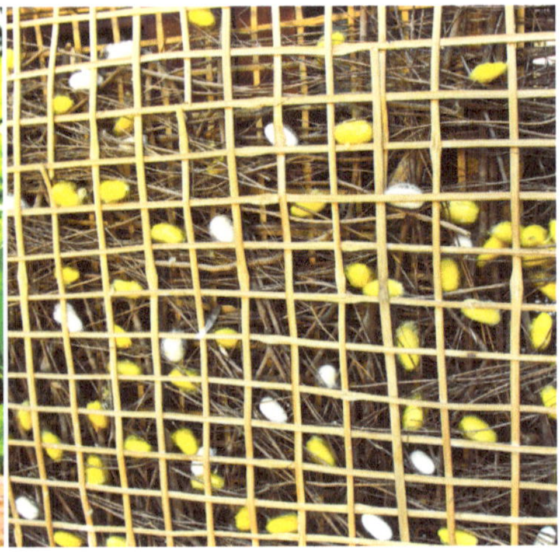

became intrigued by the silk process in **HOI AN...**

I watched a pearl gatherer meticulously removing pearls from oysters in **VIET NAM**...

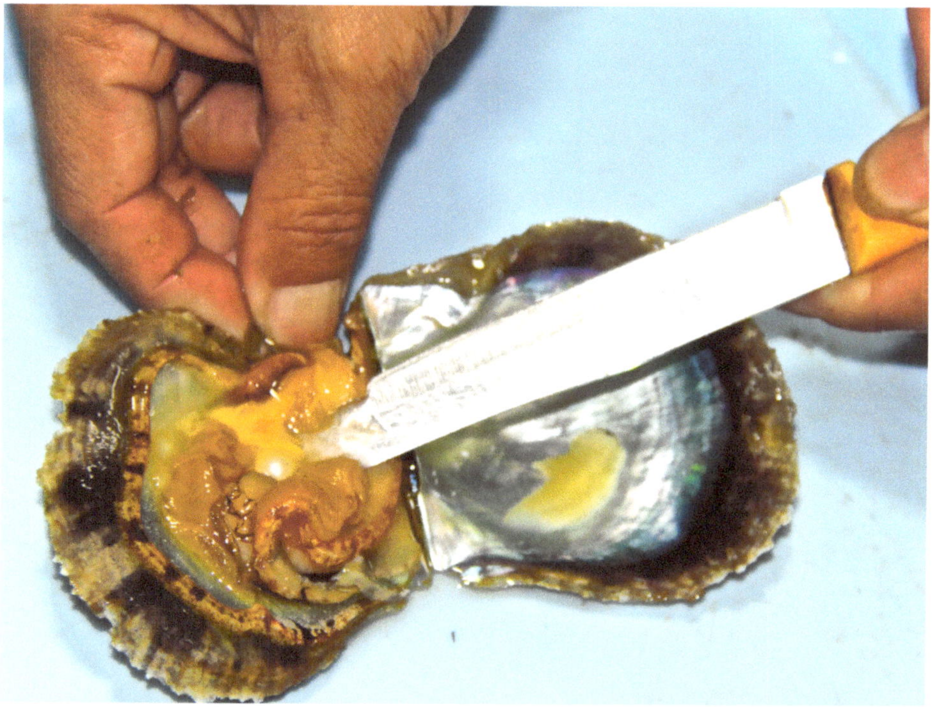

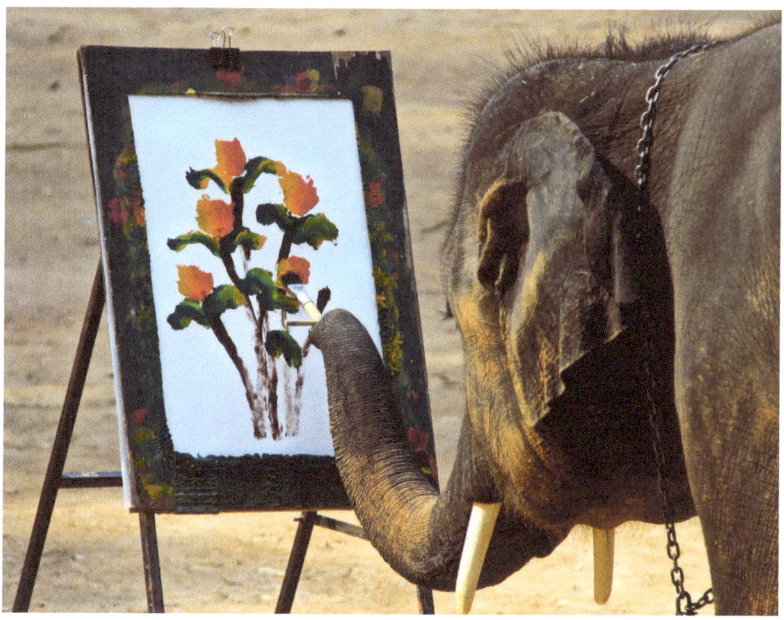

I and an elephant in **THAILAND** pick up a brush with his trunk and carefully paint a flowered picture...

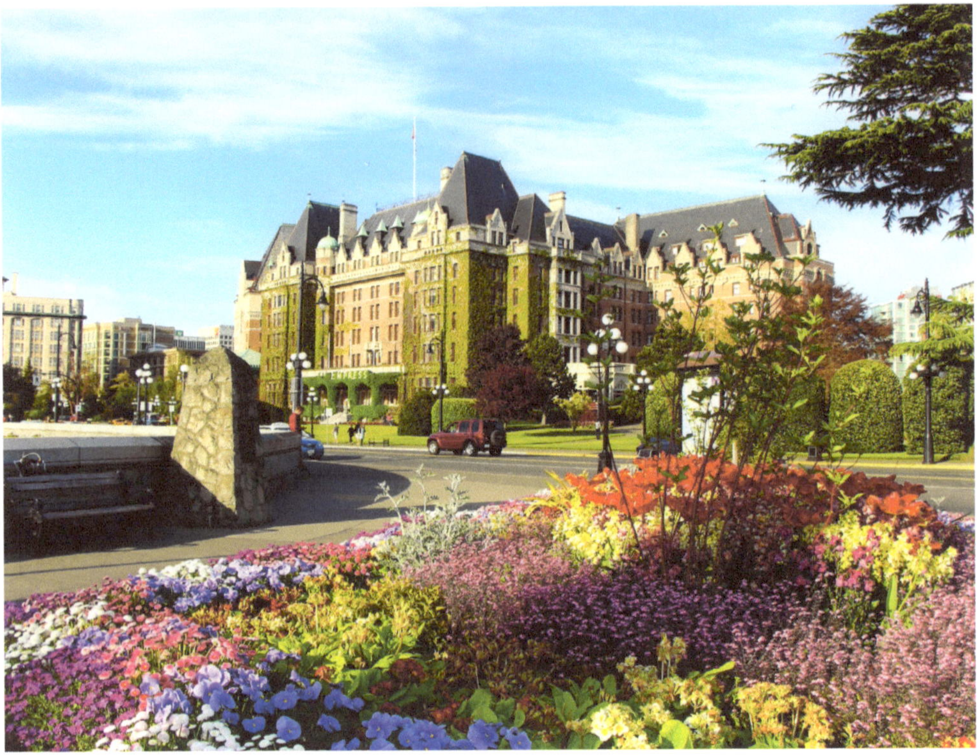

I scattered ashes of a friend among

VANCOUVER'S BEAUTIFUL GARDENS...

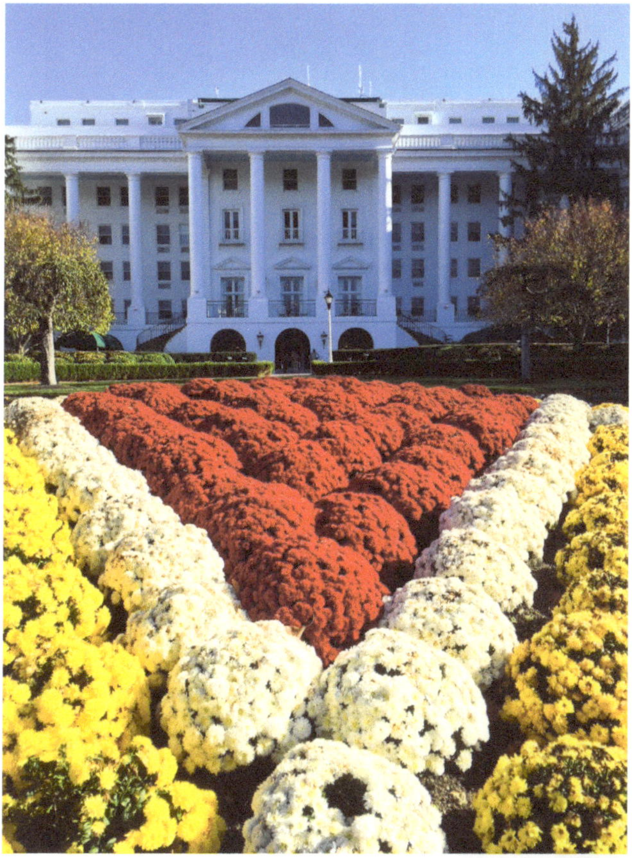

I enjoyed high tea at **THE GREENBRIER** in the mountains of **WEST VIRGINIA**...

I delighted in hot chocolate on a snowy winter day in **WYOMING'S MOUNTAINS**...

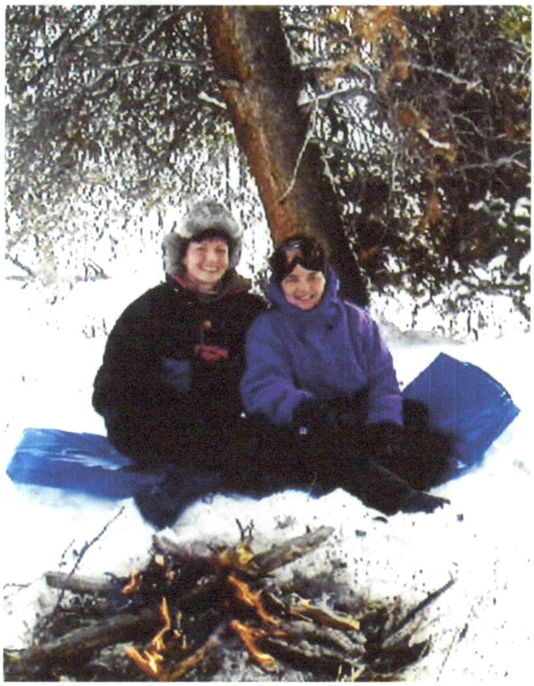

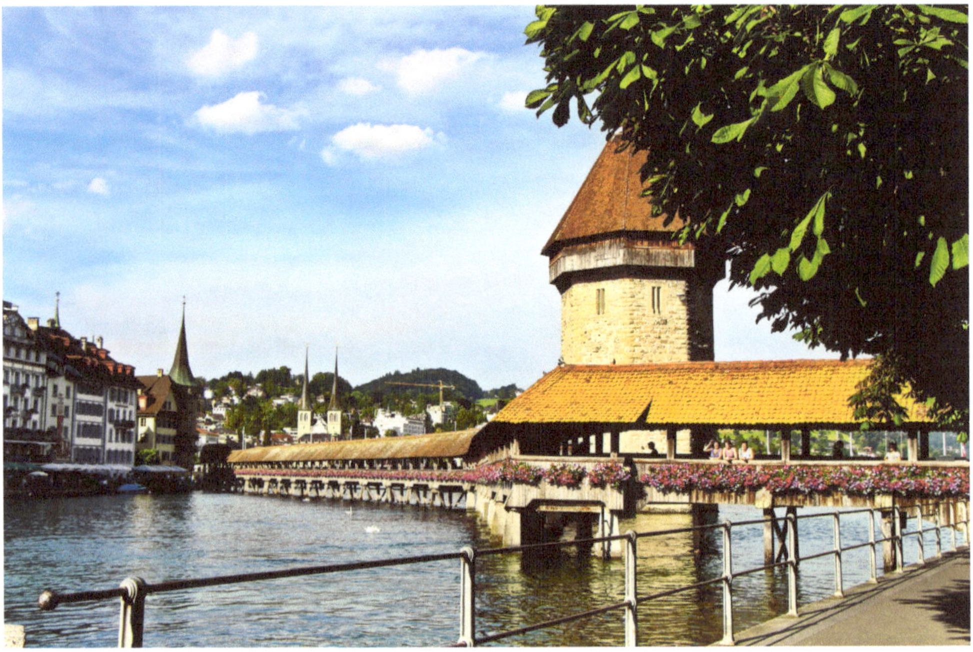

strolled through **LUCERNE'S** flower-laced Chapel Bridge...

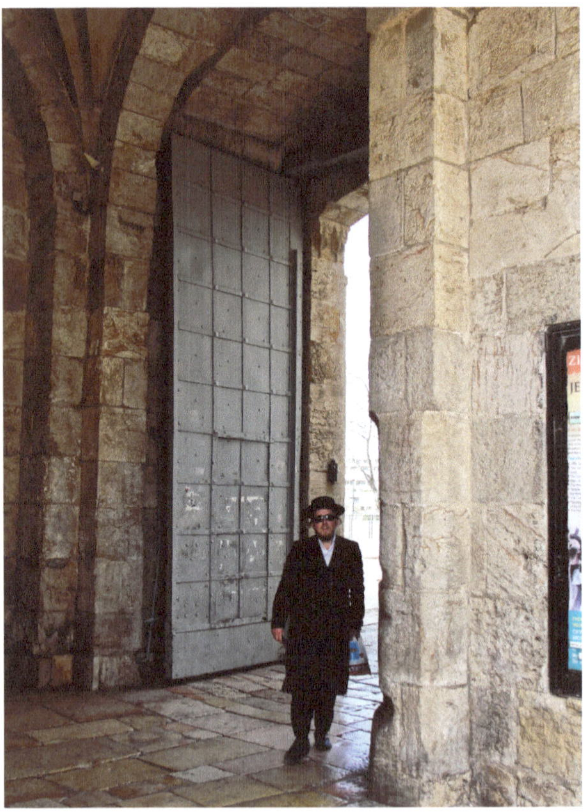

and walked the
history-laden
streets of old
JERUSALEM...

enjoyed a
SPANISH FESTIVAL
in San Diego...

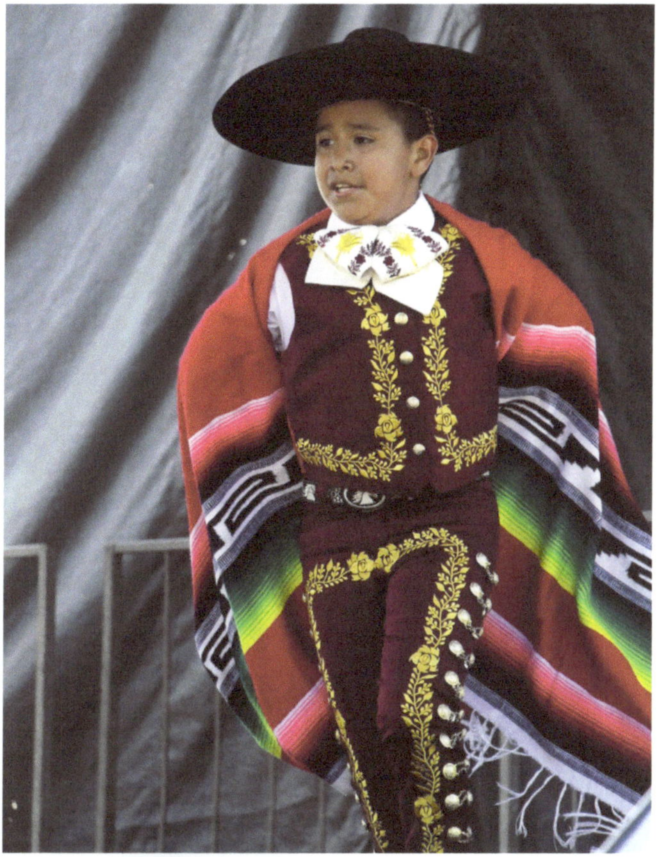

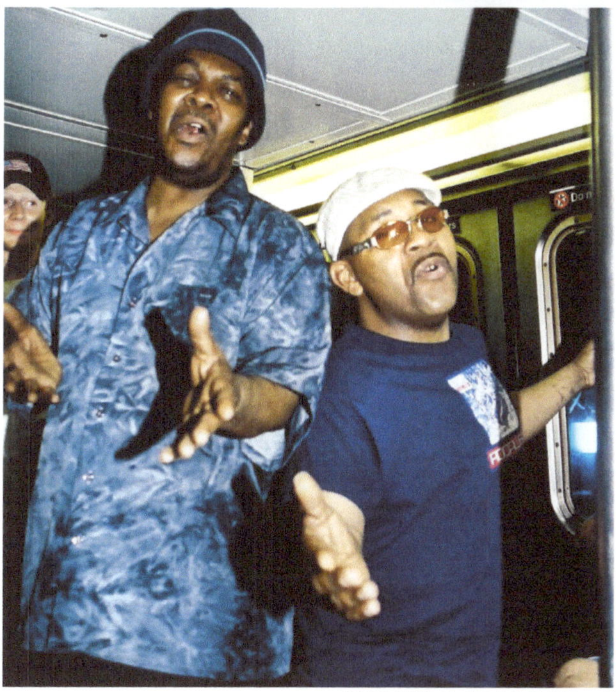

and joined the
"DOO-WOP" SINGERS on
the New York's
Subway...

were rabid fans at

COLLEGE AND PRO FOOTBALL GAMES...

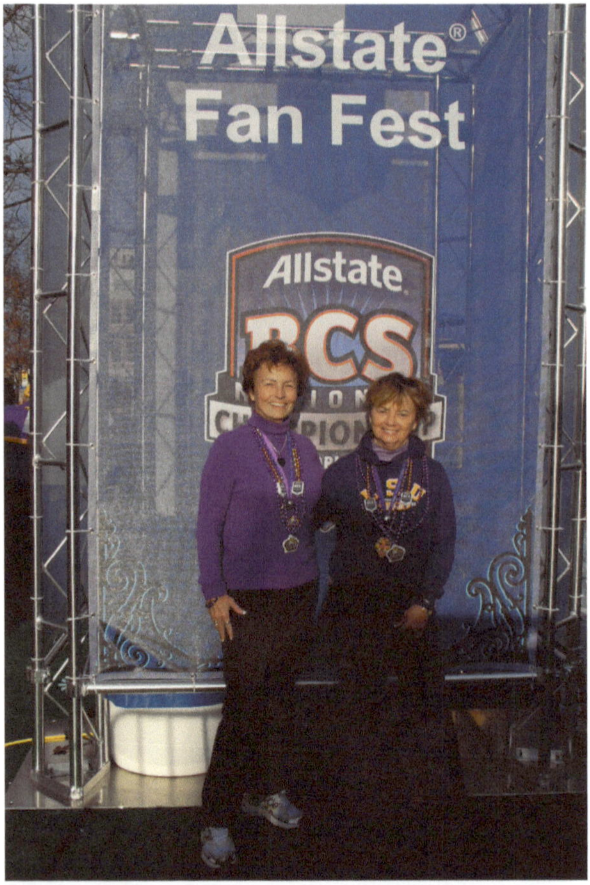

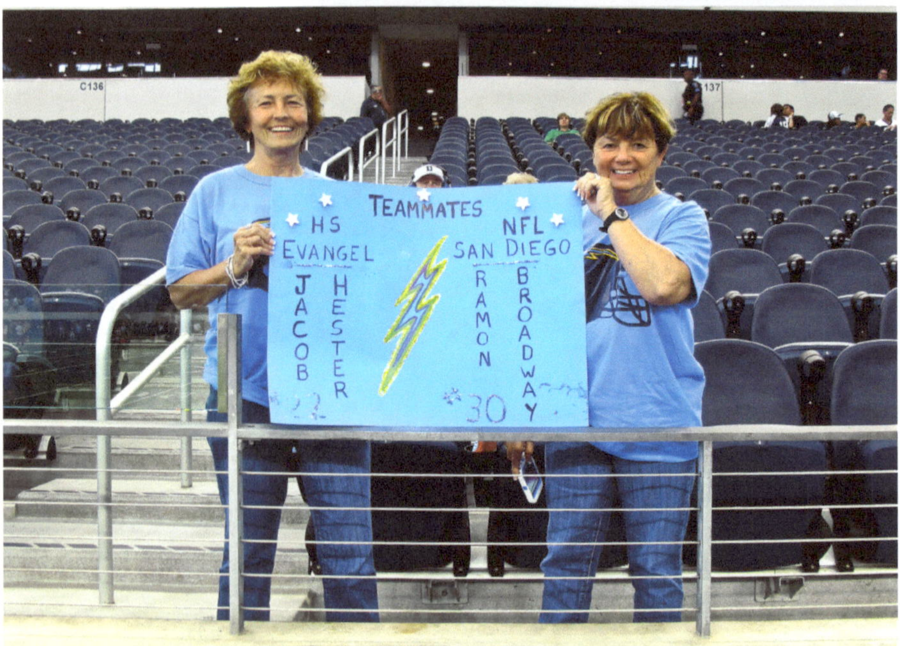

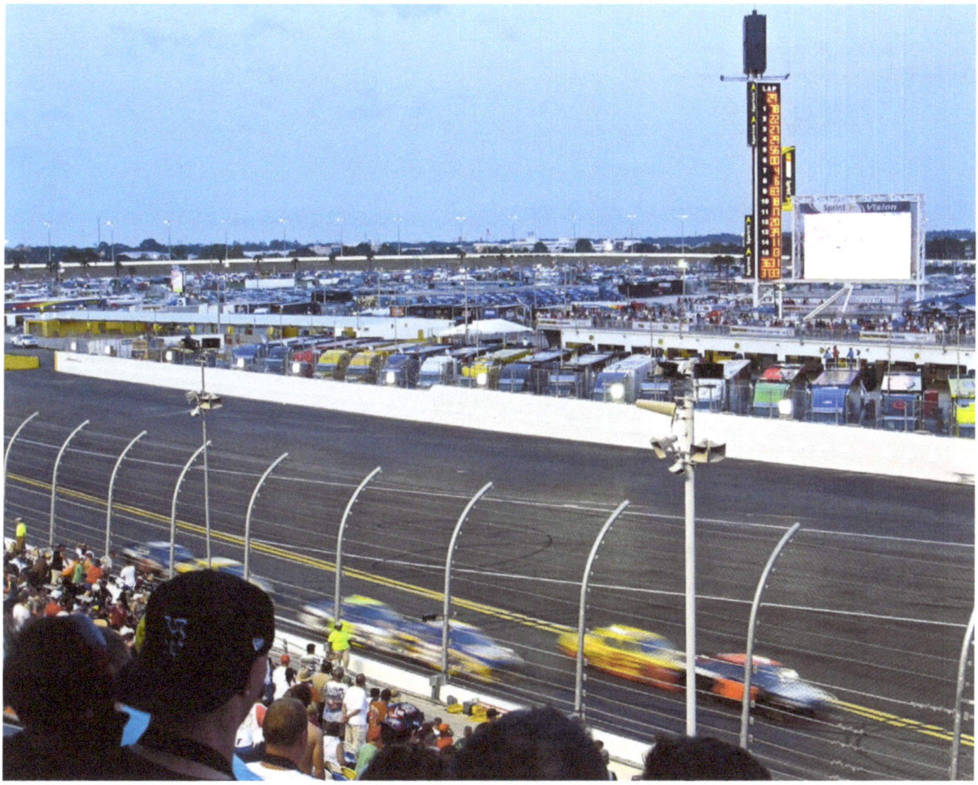

picked our favorites at the **INDY 500** & **DAYTONA SPEEDWAY**...

visited the
ST. LOUIS,
home of the famous
CLYDESDALE HORSES...

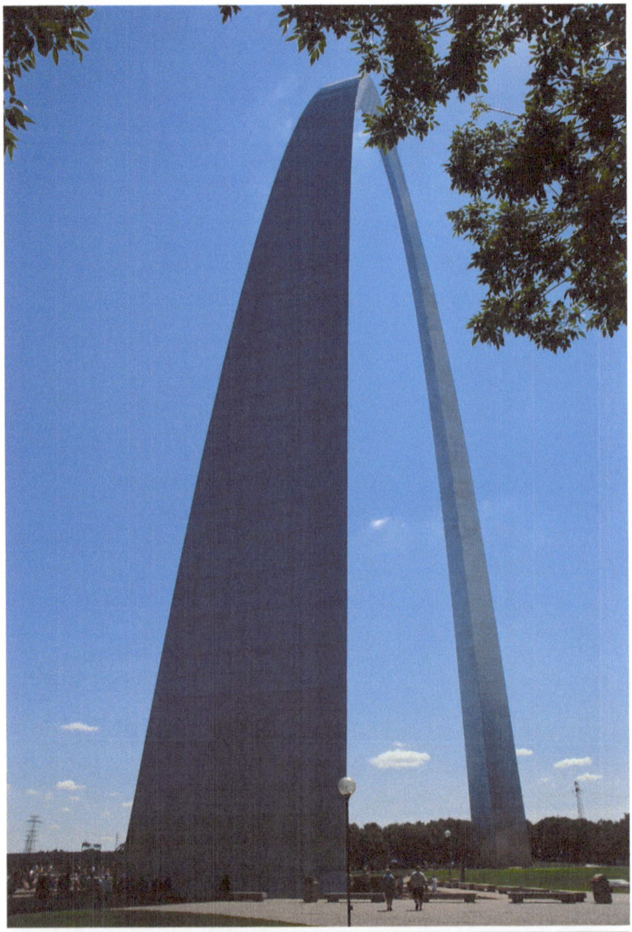

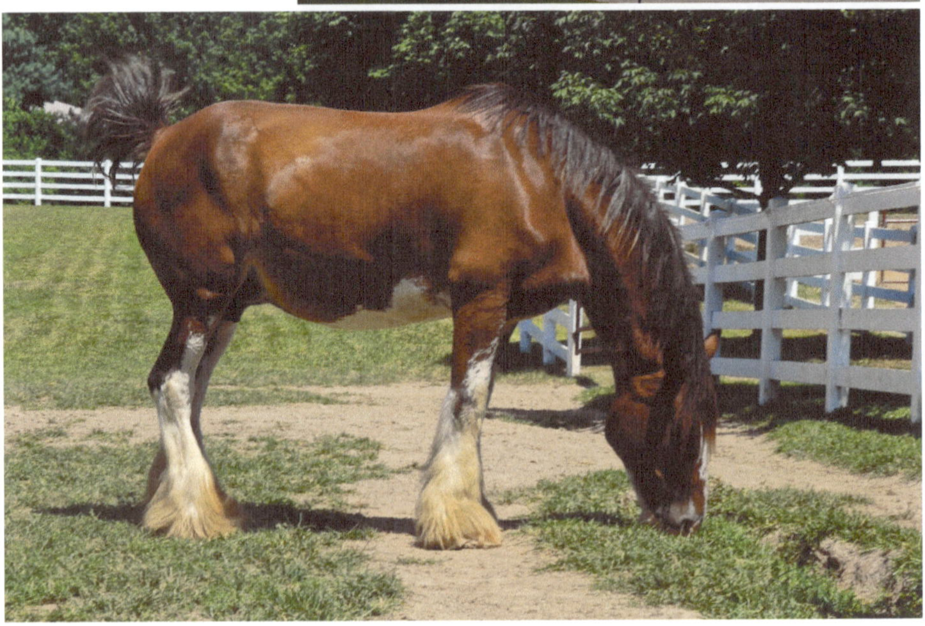

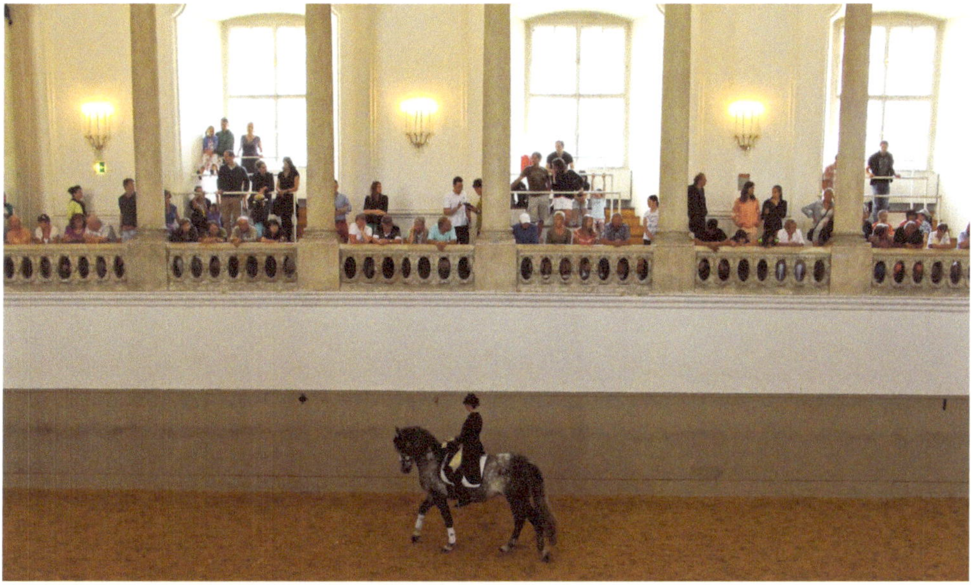

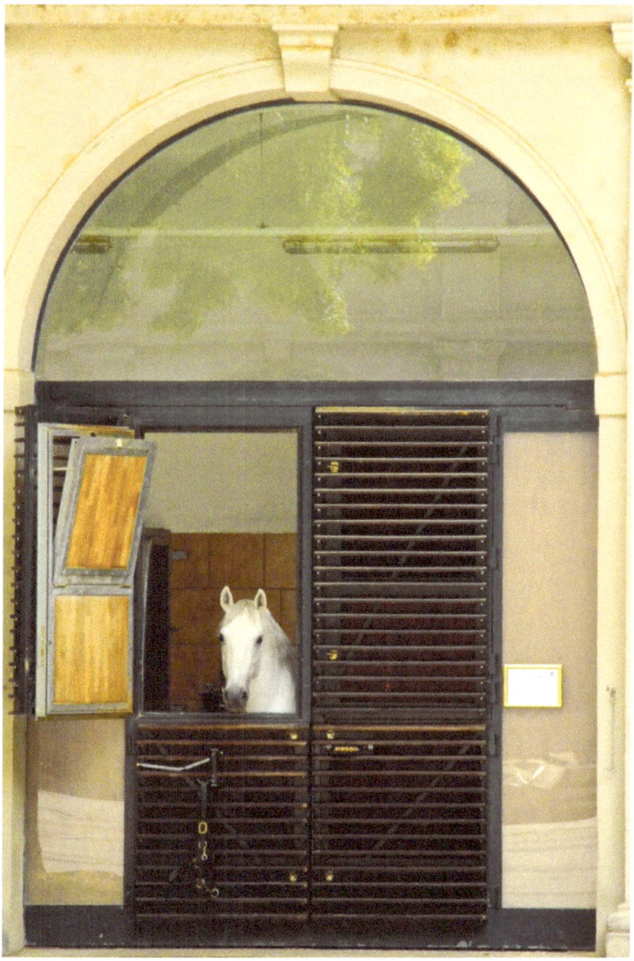

and the
world -renowned
LIPPIZANS
in Vienna...

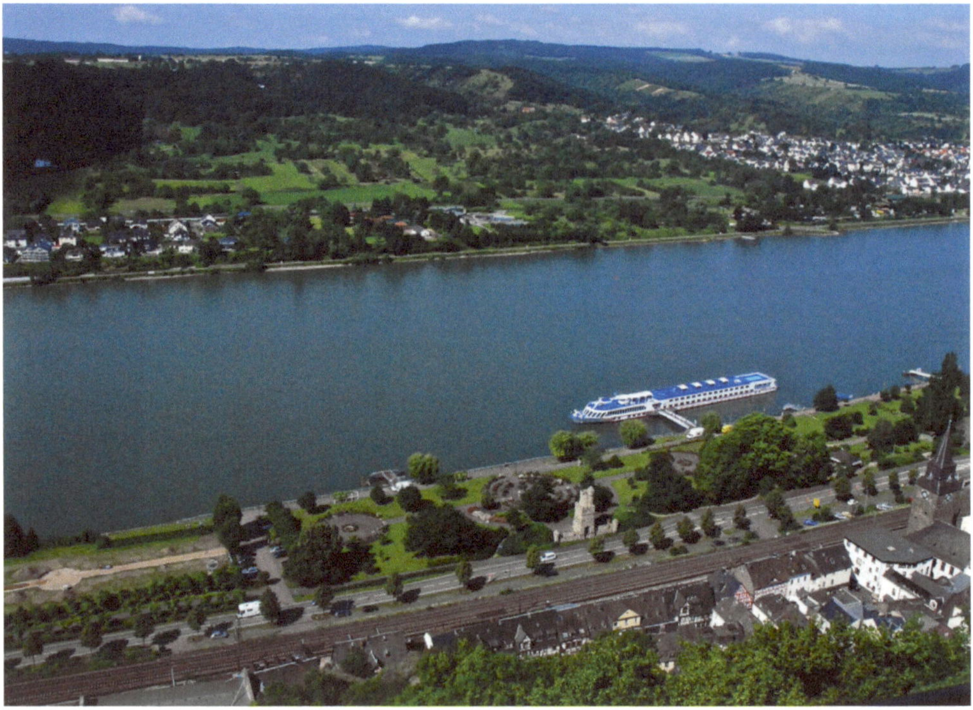

cruised Europe's **BLUE DANUBE**...

Lao's **MUDDY MEKONG**...

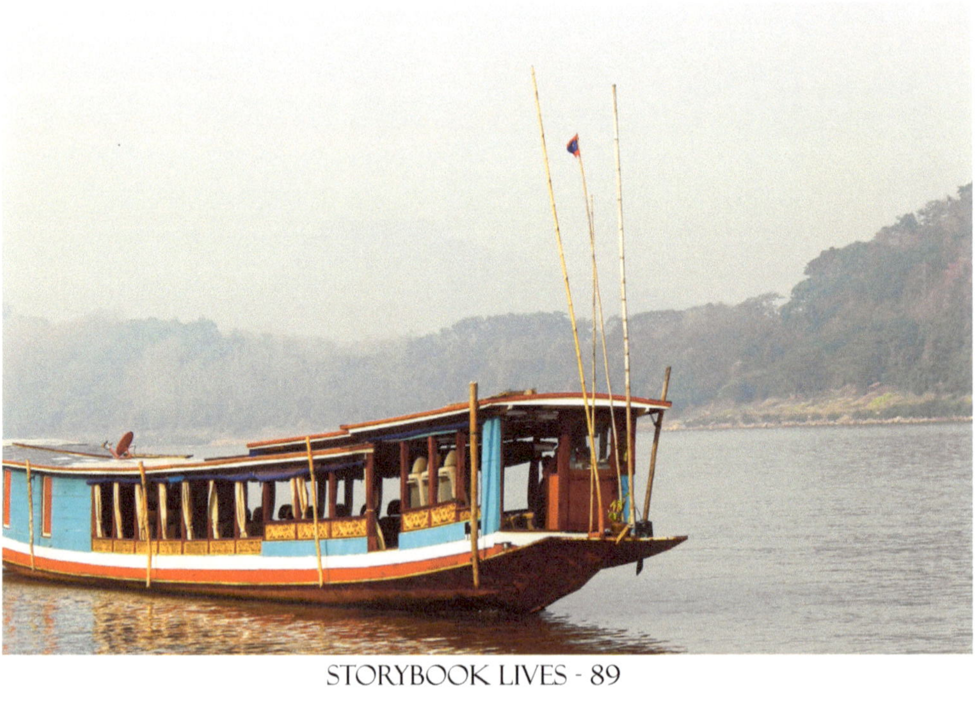

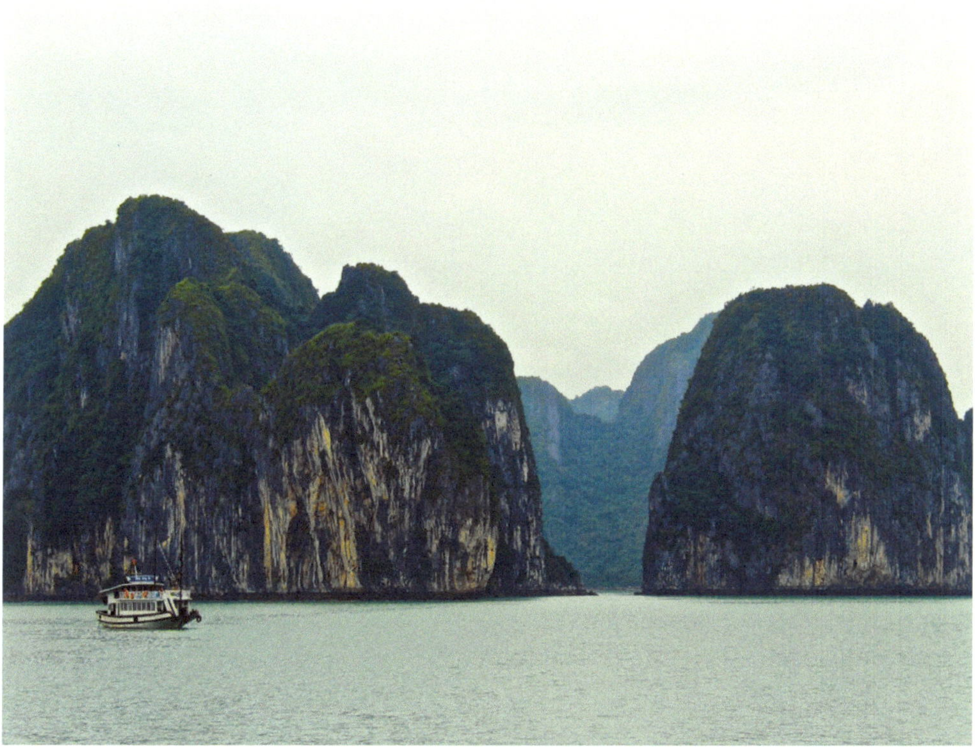

Viet Nam's limestone pillared **HA LONG BAY**...

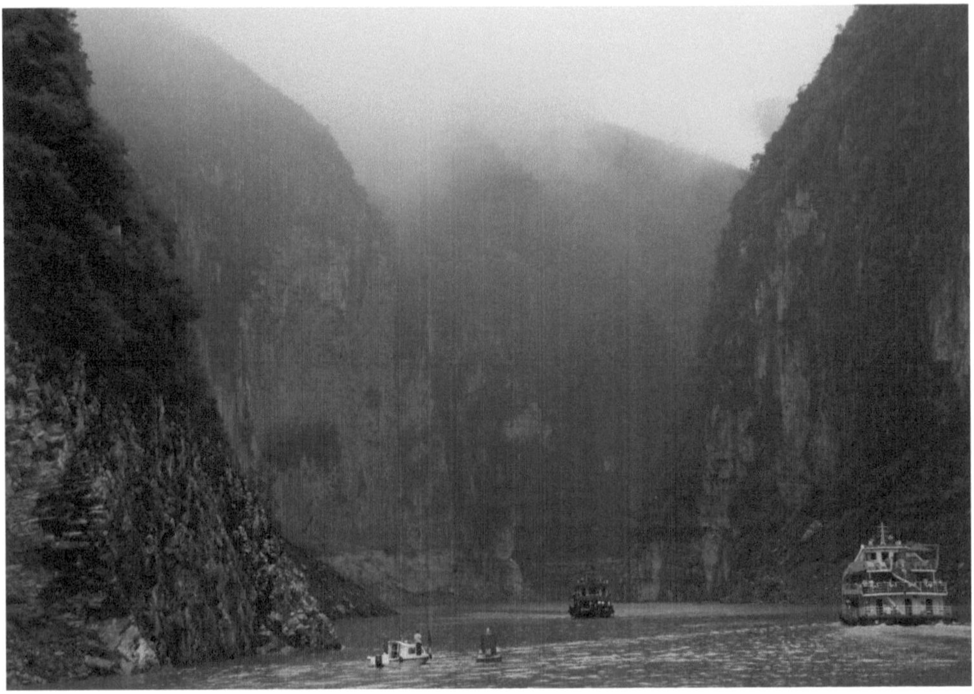

the **MISTY YANTZEE**

through the Three Gorges region...

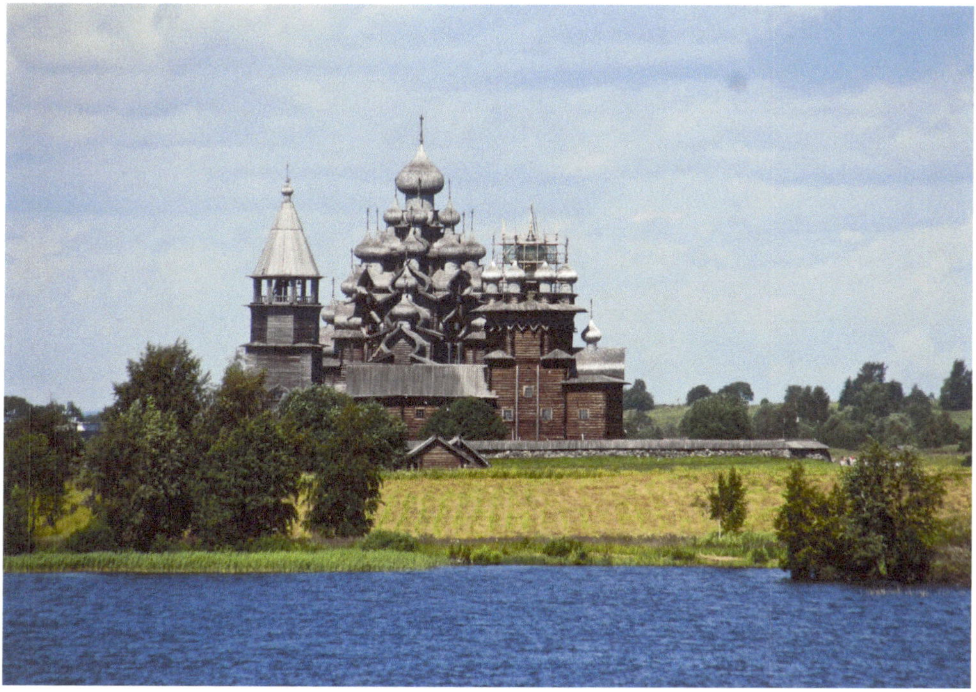

and Russia's historic **VOLGA**...

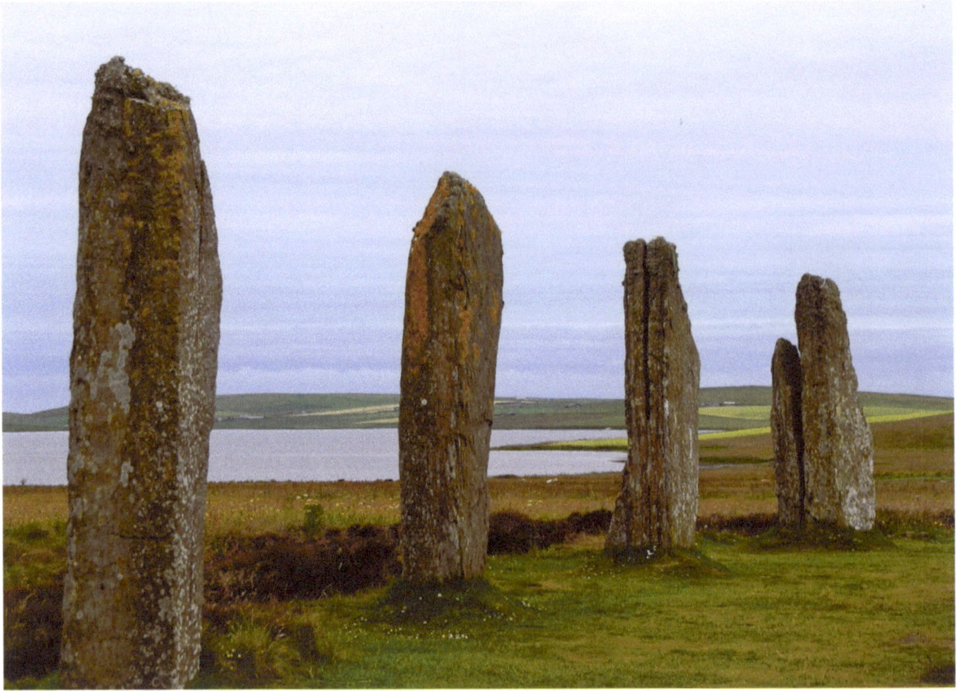

meandered through

SCOTLAND'S STONEHENGE

of the North
(actually predates
Stonehenge by
approximately
2000 years)...

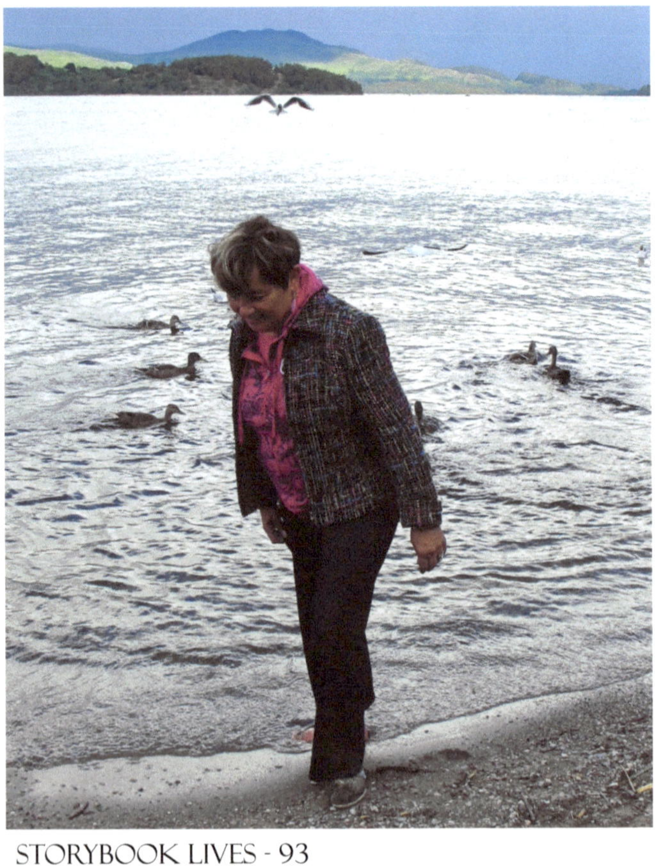

I stepped into

NESSIE'S LOCH...

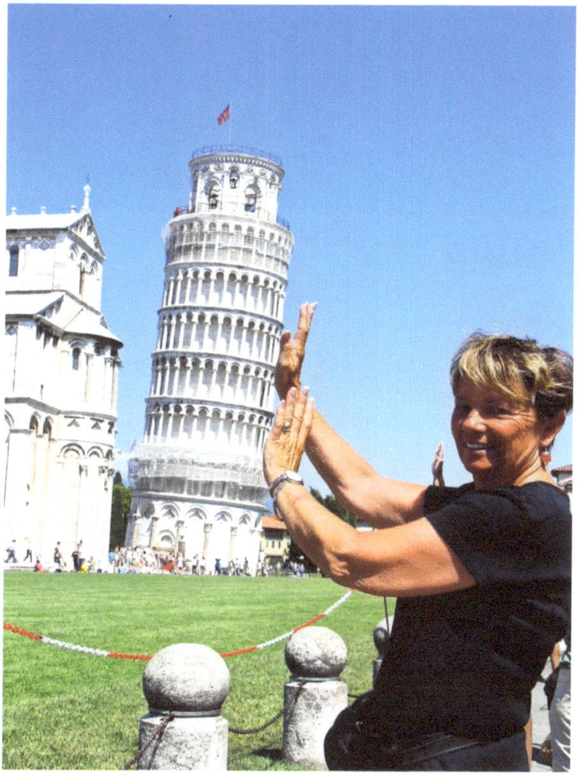

| supported the **LEANING TOWER OF PISA...**

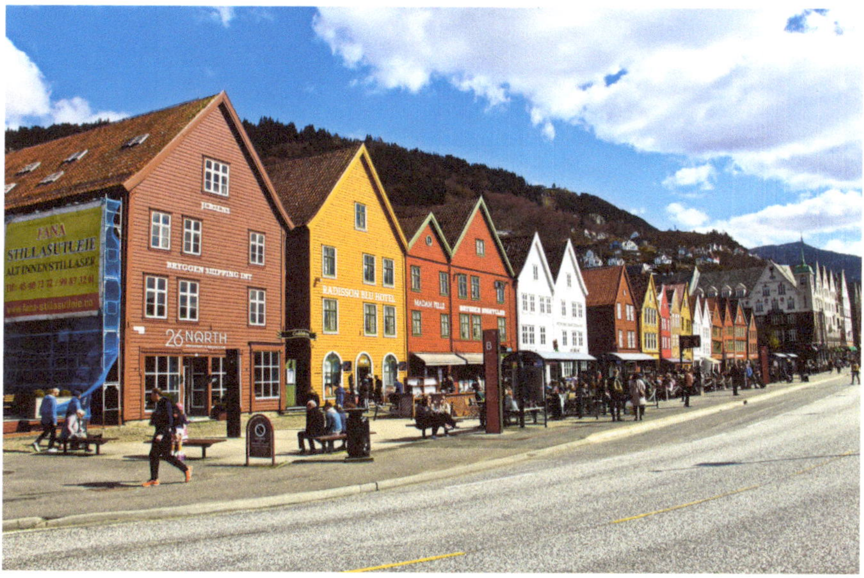

relaxed in the serenity of **BERGEN**, Norway's colorful wooden buildings, quaintly nestled in this fjord capital... **|**

were welcomed

by the leaders of

ILLFRACOMBE, ENGLAND

making history as their first cruise ship visitors...

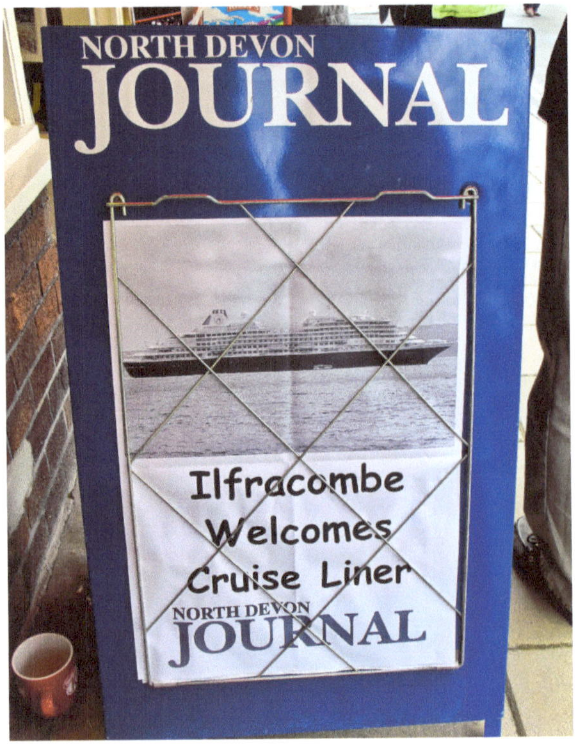

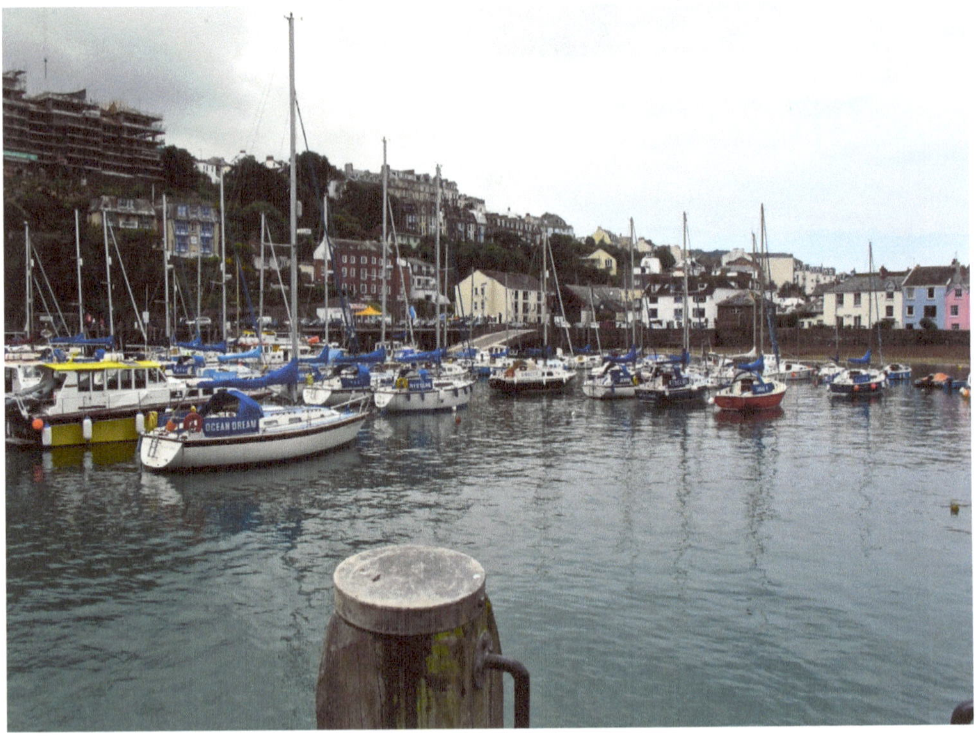

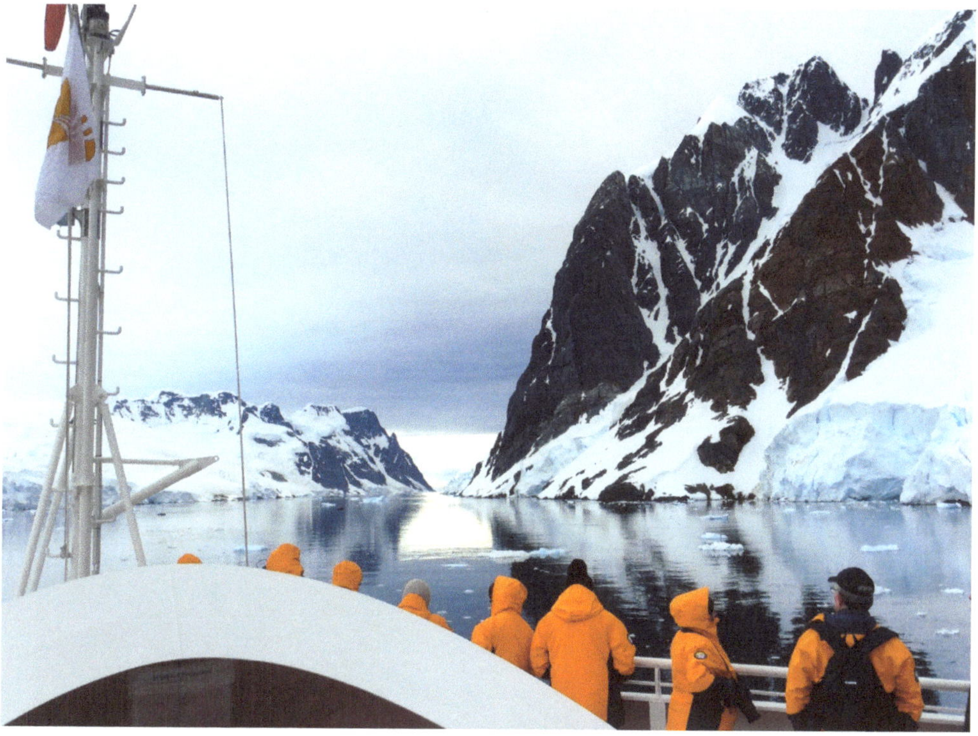

I and received a certificate acknowledging our being aboard a ship sailing further south into

ANTARCTIC WATERS

than any other ship in their fleet...

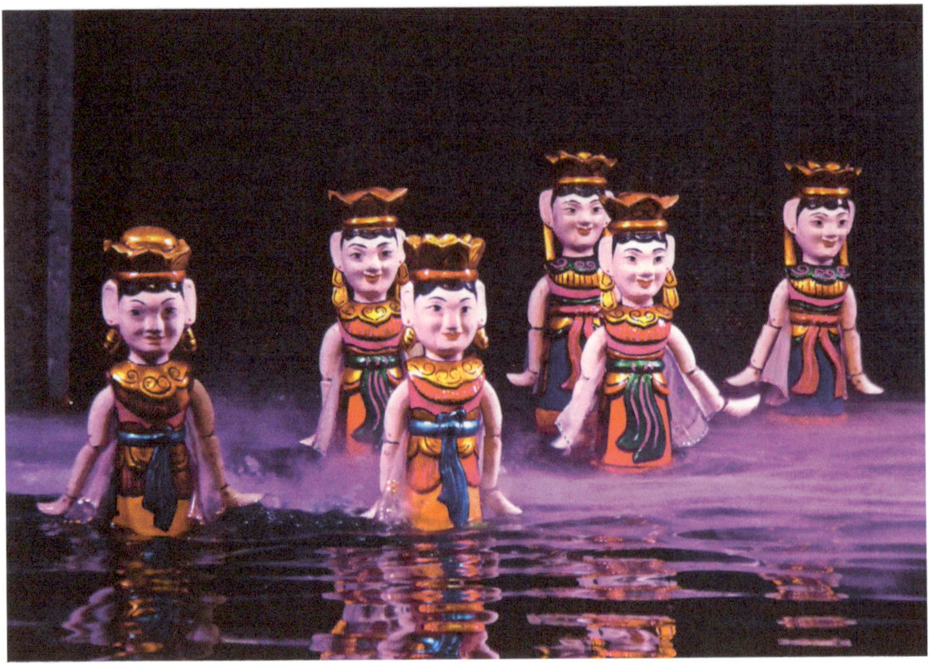

enjoyed the Vietnamese cultural displays of **WATER PUPPETS**...

the storytelling **CHINESE DANCERS**...

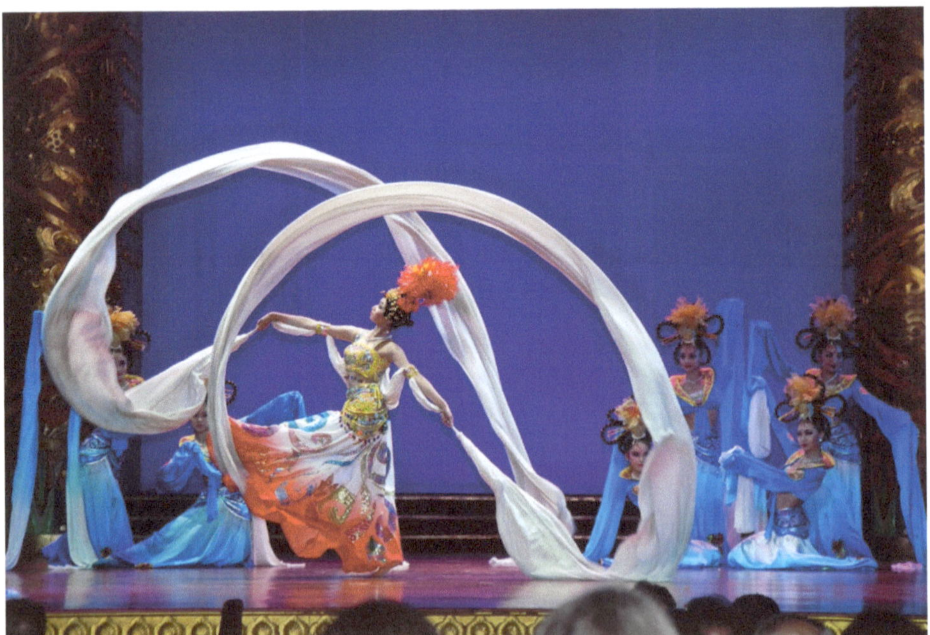

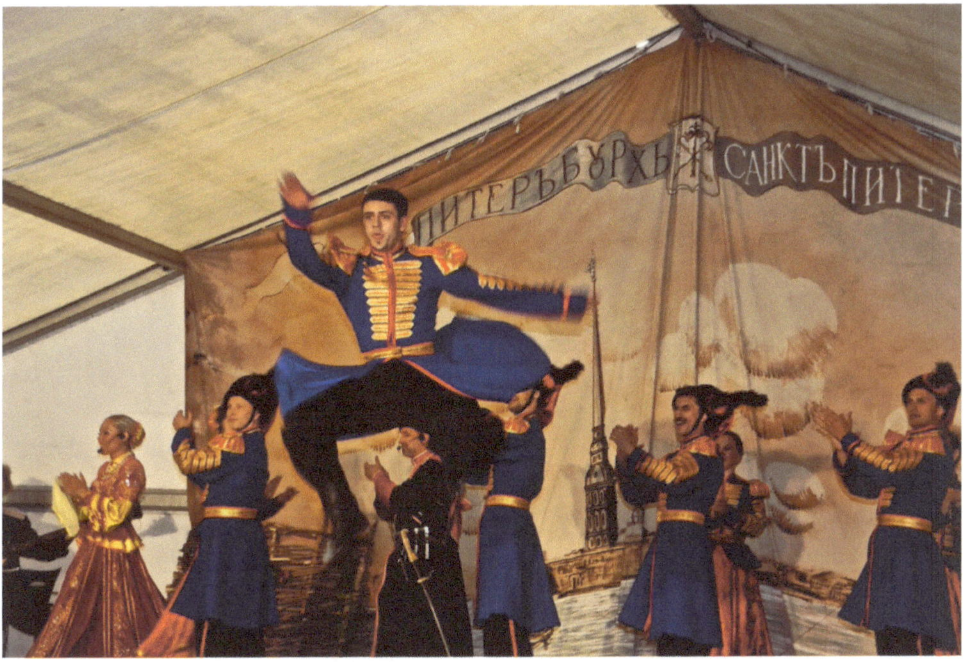

the lively **RUSSIAN PERFORMERS...**

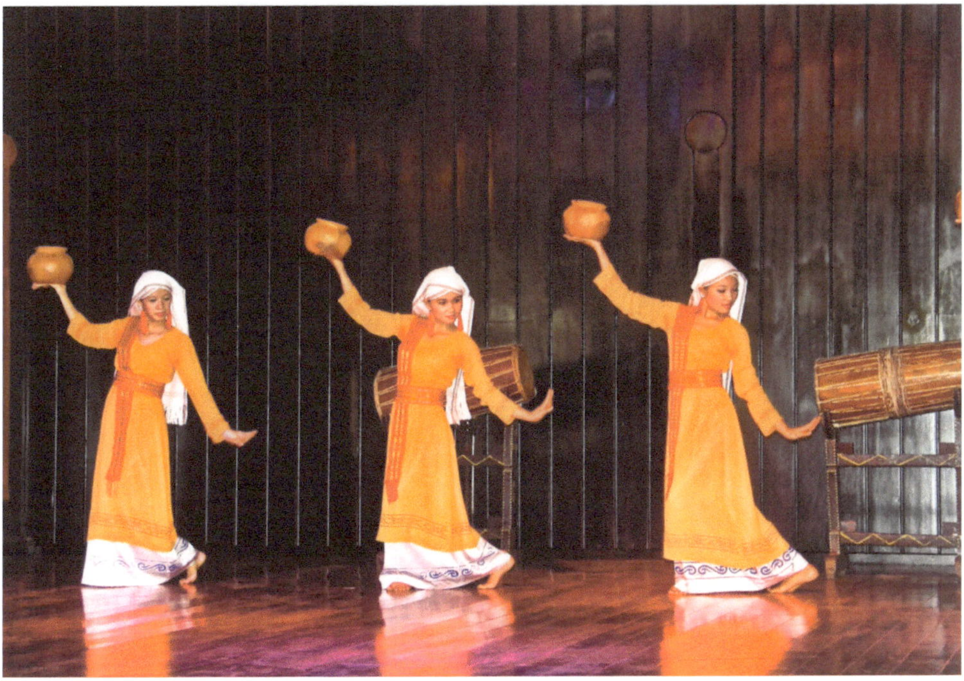

and the synchronized **SIAMESE MOVEMENTS...**

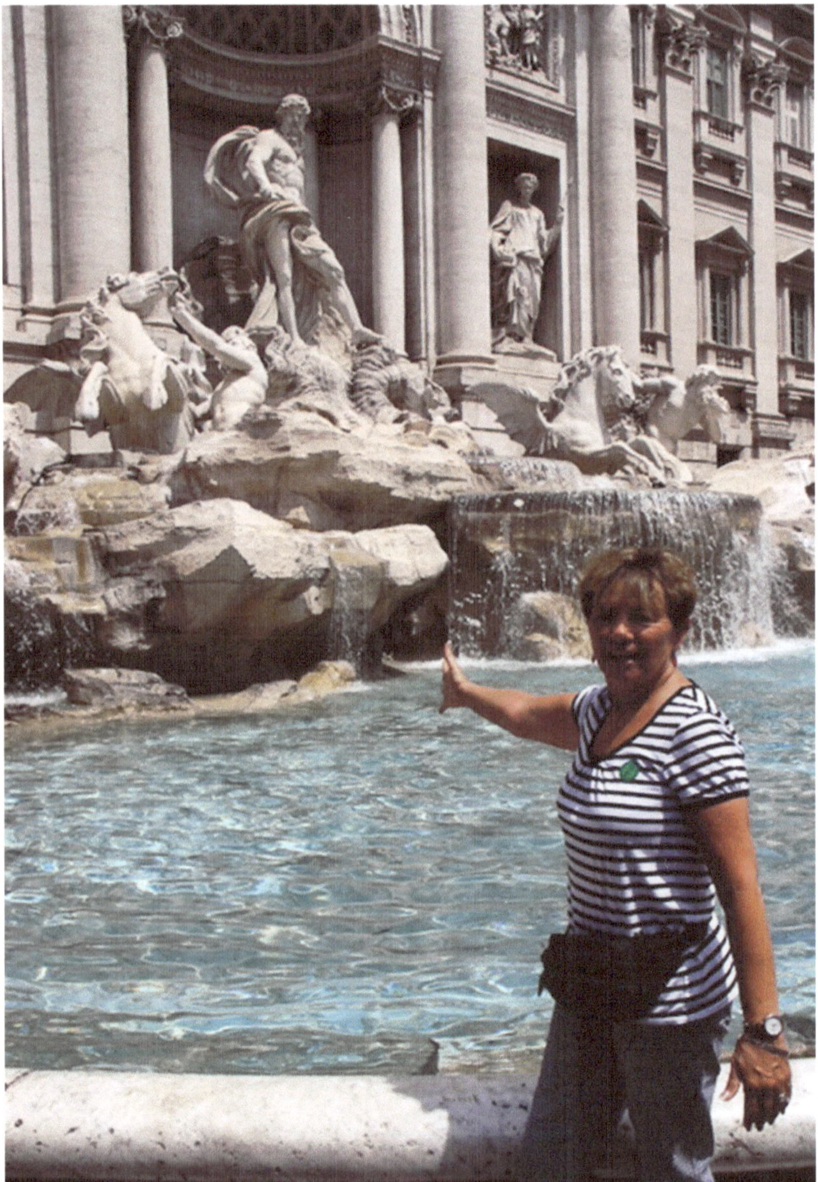

Finally, we threw coins into **TREVI FOUNTAIN**...
wishing to do it all over again!

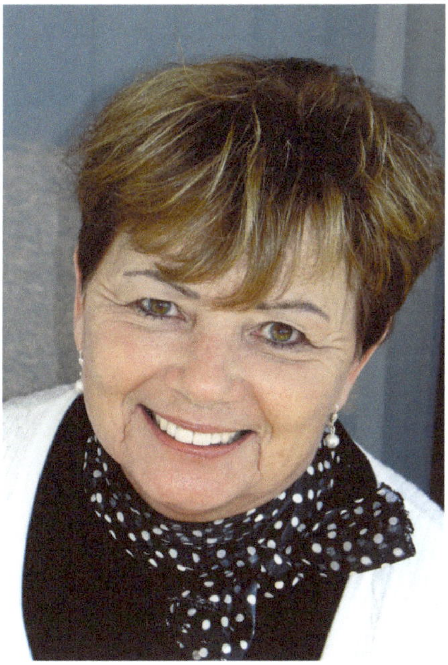

In honor of

MARTHA ELLIS

sister,

friend…

co-worker…

travel buddy…

inspiration and motivation for this book.

When someone you love becomes a memory…

that memory becomes a treasure!

ABOUT THE AUTHORS

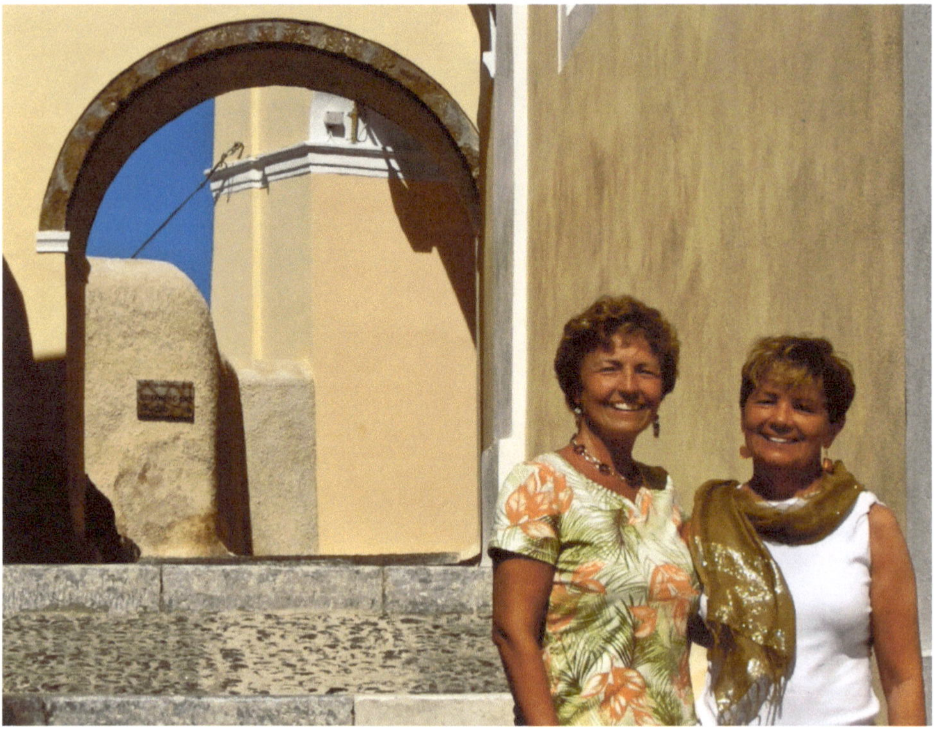

Pat Chapman and Martha Ellis, two educators, embarked on a quest that ultimately took them to all seven continents. The more they saw of this world, the more they wanted to see. The more they saw of this world, the more they wanted others to see. Their desire is that the books they have written and the photographs they have shared will offer a glimpse of the beauty and diversity of this planet as well as the sameness of its people.

Other books by Pat Chapman and Martha Ellis:

"ALPHABET ZOO"
"THEY LAUGH IN MY LANGUAGE"
"JOURNEY TO THE SEVENTH CONTINENT"

THE BLIND MEN AND THE ELEPHANT
JOHN GODFREY SAXE

I.
It was six men of Indostan To learning much inclined,
Who went to see the Elephant (Though all of them were blind).
That each by observation Might satisfy his mind.

II
The First approached the Elephant, And happening to fall
Against his broad and sturdy side, At once began to bawl,
"God bless me! – but the Elephant is very like a wall!"

III

The Second, feeling of the tusk, Cried: "Ho! –What have we here
So very round and smooth and sharp? To me, 'tis mighty clear
This wonder of an Elephant is very like a spear!"

IV
The third approached the animal, And happening to take
The squirming trunk within his hands, Thus boldly up and spake:
"I see," quoth he, "the Elephant is very like a snake!"

V
The Fourth reached out his eager hand, And felt about the knee.
"What most this wonderous beast is like is mighty plain," quoth he:
"Tis clear enough the Elephant is very like a tree!"

VI
The Fifth, who chanced to touch the ear, Said: "E'en the blindest man
Can tell what this resembles most: Deny the fact who can,
This marvel of an Elephant is very like a fan!"

VII
The Sixth no sooner had begun About the beast to grope,
Than, seizing on the swinging tail That fell within his scope,
"I see," quoth he, "the Elephant is very like a rope!"

VIII
And so these men of Indostan Disputed loud and long,
Each in his own opinion Exceeding stiff and strong,
Though each was partly in the right, And all were in the wrong.

The world, like the elephant in the poem, is often only experienced from
a limited spectrum, leaving us with distorted views of the whole.
By sharing glimpses of our experiences across the seven continents,
we invite the reader to make a choice
take a chance
create a lifetime of memories...of

THIS WONDERFUL WORLD!

www.ingramcontent.com/pod-product-compliance
Ingram Content Group UK Ltd.
Pitfield, Milton Keynes, MK11 3LW, UK
UKHW061023310726
14090UKWH00023B/42